THE ZODIAC LIFE PATH

A COSMIC GUIDE TO FINDING TRUE LOVE, HEALING YOURSELF, AND LIVING YOUR LIFE'S PURPOSE

NINA STERLE

THOUGHT
CATALOG
Books
THOUGHTCATALOG.COM

Copyright © 2025 Nina Sterle.

All rights reserved. No part of this book may be reproduced or transmitted in any form or any means, electronic or mechanical, without prior written consent and permission from Thought Catalog.

Published by Thought Catalog Books, an imprint of Thought Catalog, a digital magazine owned and operated by The Thought & Expression Co. Inc., an independent media organization founded in 2010 and based in the United States of America. For stocking inquiries, contact stockists@shopcatalog.com.

thoughtcatalog.com | shopcatalog.com

Printed internationally by Amazon.

ISBN 978-1-965820-16-2

LOVE & SOULMATES
7

WEALTH & FINANCES
49

BREAKUPS & HEALING
65

MANIPULATION & TOXIC RELATIONSHIPS
81

DREAMS, SUBCONSCIOUS, & THE FUTURE
101

HEALTH & WELLNESS
133

SPIRITUALITY
149

PERSONALITY
219

TRAVEL & ADVENTURE
269

ASTROLOGICAL EVENTS & HOLIDAYS
295

AFTERWORD
311

Dear reader,

If this book has reached you, it is a clear sign that you are looking to learn more—about yourself, your life, your past, and even your future. Consider this book as a compendium of zodiac- and tarot-related topics; it is not the be-all end-all that will tell your fortune based on your birthday or the tarot cards you pull, but rather a guide to help you learn, grow, and achieve your fullest life. This is the meaning behind being a practicing zodiac. None of us have it all figured out, but we must try regardless; try to please our mind, our body, our soul; try to fulfill our life's purpose; try to heal and grow no matter the obstacles standing before us. We are never complete; we are always, always practicing.

In this book, you will find 10 sections, each dedicated to a different subject. Within these sections will be the guides that I find have helped others the most—from finding a true soulmate to breaking free of your past wounds. Each section lightly touches on the subject at hand, covering everything you want to know about what your zodiac sign means and why you've pulled the tarot cards you hold. These sections are the key to unlocking the secrets of your life—little things about you that you never thought of before, but that just make so much sense when you first read them. Your dreams, your psyche, your subconscious desires, your greatest weaknesses and your truest loves—all of these things can be unlocked within these pages.

I hope this book helps you on your journey as a practicing zodiac. No matter whether you are just beginning to learn about astrology or are deep into your astrological journey, we are all always learning, growing, and moving forward—joined by a singular practice under the guidance of the stars.

With love and gratitude,
Nina

LOVE & SOULMATES

Your guide to finding the one you're meant to be with, no matter your star sign.

THESE ZODIAC SIGNS ARE THE MOST CAUTIOUS WHEN IT COMES TO ROMANCE

TAURUS

As someone who loves staying within their comfort zone, you tend to look at romance with a level head, Taurus. You often retain your ability to determine whether or not a person is right for you from an objective perspective—even if romance is involved. When you open yourself up to someone, you want to make sure that they're safe to trust. As a grounded person, you tend to keep a smaller social circle (and your sign can often be introverted, too), so you want to ensure you're letting the right people into your life no matter what.

CANCER

You love making new connections and opening up to people, Cancer. It's part of who you are—someone who loves caring for others and nurturing them, too. You're a sensitive soul, but that doesn't always mean you rush into romance. Sometimes you get a little caught up in the chemicals and romantic fantasies with another person (and you might even fall victim to toxic relationships if you struggle with setting boundaries). But because you're empathetic and sensitive, you also try to be cautious when connecting with someone new. It's a good way of protecting yourself and your precious energy.

VIRGO

As someone who's organized and methodical, you tend to take a more cautious approach to dating. You don't want to make any serious decisions too soon, and you always take your time to get to know people in an honest, authentic way. You want to connect with people in a manner that shows your full self (and vice versa) so that you can find your absolute best match. You approach dating in a way that's just as organized as the rest of your life is—and though you might move slowly, you often see a lot of benefit from it.

CAPRICORN

As a sign who's known for overthinking, you tend to be cautious when it comes to romance. You're a loyal sign who takes love seriously, but you're also relatively logical, so you like to be realistic about dating. You don't tend to rush into relationships or move too quickly when getting to know someone. Capricorns also tend to look for more serious relationships, which could mean that you like to vet your prospects long-term to make sure you'll have a healthy, stable relationship together. Plus, since you're prone to thinking things through a little too often, it's no surprise that you approach romance slowly and with some hesitation.

WHAT YOUR PARTNER LIKES ABOUT YOU, BASED ON YOUR ZODIAC SIGN

ARIES: YOUR AMBITION

As the sign that never sleeps, one thing your romantic partner is probably attracted to is your sense of ambition. You have a drive that constantly pushes you forward—you're always growing and developing in new ways, which is an admirable trait for any romantic interest to have. There's nothing better than someone who is confident in themselves and dedicated to their own goals.

TAURUS: YOUR STABILITY

Given your love of comfort and routine, your partner is likely attracted to the fact that you present yourself with a boatload of stability. You're reliable and grounded, and you're generally a peaceful person to be around. Your partner probably appreciates the fact that you'll always be there for them—the chance to feel truly secure in a relationship is a wonderful thing.

GEMINI: YOUR WONDER

Of course you're a curious sign, Gemini—but it's the fact that you never fail to find little things to admire each day that inspires your partner the most. The passion you have for your latest favorite interest or hobby just can't be matched, and you often draw other people into your interests through sheer excitement. It's more than contagious enough to bring your partner joy, too.

CANCER: YOUR SENSITIVITY

As someone who truly wears their heart on their sleeve, it's likely that your partner appreciates the fact that you're a sensitive soul. Your empathy and care for your loved ones probably brings your partner a lot of happiness, and the fact that you're an emotional person likely matches well with your partner's own emotional intellect, too.

LEO: YOUR GENEROSITY

Though your sign is known for being dramatic and loving attention, your sign is also hailed as one of the more generous signs of the zodiac. When isn't this an attractive trait to have? Whether you're giving to a close friend or helping out someone you've never even met before, your partner really admires your generosity in all situations—after all, it's the sign of a good soul.

VIRGO: YOUR RESPONSIBILITY

Is your partner as mature as you are, Virgo? Whether they are or not, they probably appreciate your responsibility more than you know. Your preparedness, your attention to fine detail, and all your little quirks and minor obsessions over your daily lives—you might be used to it, but your partner probably remembers how disorganized things were before you came around. Or maybe they just appreciate the opportunity to plan your schedules in tandem.

LIBRA: YOUR SENSE OF VALUES

As the judicial side of the zodiac, it's probably not much of a surprise to hear that your partner appreciates the fact that you stick to your morals. But having strong values that you don't compromise on can be an attractive trait to have. Your partner is likely to appreciate the fact that you know exactly what you stand for and why, and that you're ready to defend what's right.

SCORPIO: YOUR AUTHENTICITY

You're a person who likes to be genuine—when you've truly connected with someone, you want to know them on a deeper level (and might even start taking your own walls down, too). This is something about you that your partner can't help but appreciate. When someone takes time to get to know you in a genuine way, it makes the relationship feel deeper and more real. This makes your connection to your partner completely unique.

SAGITTARIUS: YOUR INDEPENDENCE

You value your independence intensely—as someone who can't help but prioritize freedom, independence is something you seek in a relationship. But your partner probably likes that about you, too—the fact that you have your own interests and passions, your own goals to pursue, and can stand as a complete person outside of the relationship can be immensely attractive.

CAPRICORN: YOUR MATURITY

You provide a stable ground for your partner to land on, Capricorn. Even if you do tend to overthink sometimes, you approach each challenge with a level head and a disciplined mind. There's no doubt that's an impressive skill, and your partner is likely to appreciate your sense of maturity. From your personal values to your goals and achievements, your partner knows they can rely on you.

AQUARIUS: YOUR QUIRKINESS

You probably already know that you're the quirkiest sign of the zodiac, Aquarius. Of course your partner would like that about you. Whether it's your sense of style, your living space, your work, or just your personality, there are bound to be plenty of quirky things about you for your partner to enjoy. They probably also love participating in hobbies with you or listening to you talk about your latest interests.

PISCES: YOUR IMAGINATION

Has your partner taken a unique interest in your creativity, Pisces? No surprises there—it's your imagination that never fails to impress them. This applies to your work, your hobbies, and even the basic thoughts you express to your partner. Whether you're dreaming up a new date idea or showing off your latest creative project, it's your endless imagination and creativity that impresses your partner most.

THESE 3 ZODIAC SIGNS ARE WEIRDLY GOOD WITH PICKUP LINES

SCORPIO

Scorpio is easily one of the most magnetic and charming signs in the zodiac. This makes them great with pretty much any kind of introduction in the social scene—even if it's a cringey pickup line that wouldn't work on most people. They know when (and how) to play things off like a joke and how to riff off of others' responses, making them more memorable and easier to talk to. They're socially charming enough that you'd likely never find Scorpio resorting to pickup lines in public, but if you double-dog dared them, they might just impress you with a smooth pickup line every now and again.

LEO

Leo is good with pickup lines because they're extremely confident and tend to follow through on anything they try. They'll give you a horrible pickup line with a straight face and no hint of anxiety, and that kind of leadership makes them interesting no matter what. They also know how to laugh at themselves for the sake of their audience, making them charming no matter who they're talking to. Their love of attention and performance means that they'll give a perfect recitation of any pickup line with incredible theatrics.

GEMINI

Gemini is a naturally sociable and lovable sign. If they give you a pickup line, it will likely be easy for you to laugh along and keep talking to Gemini—their charm is very natural, making it easy for the two of you to hold a conversation. They know how to keep things from getting awkward and how to charm a crowd, which makes them seem more desirable. Even if they're using a cheesy pickup line, they're socially intelligent enough to make it seem like a quirkily charming irony.

HOW TO KEEP YOUR RELATIONSHIP EXCITING, BASED ON THEIR ZODIAC SIGN

ARIES: FRIENDLY COMPETITION

The hardest part about friendly competition for Aries is going to be keeping things friendly, but I think the two of you can manage it. For Aries, a little bit of competition can be really fun—even if you're not in a particularly competitive relationship. The two of you might really enjoy activities that bring a little bit of gentle competition: think board games, video games, outdoor sports, or even things like reading or cooking challenges. Just remember that the real prize isn't winning—it's building a stronger bond between the two of you.

TAURUS: ADDING SMALL THINGS TO YOUR SCHEDULE

Taurus loves routine, but this can sometimes make things feel a little monotonous. That's perfectly fine in a long-term relationship, but if you're looking to try and make things more exciting for them, you can help Taurus shift out of their comfort zone without disrupting the sanctity of your date nights. It's a bad thing to spring a huge surprise on Taurus, but you might enjoy both changing things up a little occasionally—trying new restaurants, new driving routes to your usual spots, or even planning an activity the two of you have never done before.

GEMINI: LEARNING NEW TOPICS

Gemini loves learning—the most exciting thing to them is something their curiosity can grapple with for a while. You'll never lose their interest if you present them with new topics to think about—especially if the two of you agree to a friendly debate or discussion. You might enjoy watching an interesting documentary, buddy reading a book, or joining a new interest club. It's also important for the two of you to discuss what you're learning one on one for a little extra bonding time.

CANCER: USING SENTIMENTALITY

To keep things interesting with Cancer, you might want to try planning things around favorite memories of yours. That doesn't mean you have to constantly repeat old dates, but Cancer will always appreciate things like love letters, printed photos of activities you went to together, or playlists of songs that remind you of them. They'd also love it if you surprised them with a trip to a spot that's meaningful to the two of you or put a new twist on old favorite activities together—think going on a sailing tour if you first met at the beach, taking a mixology class at your favorite bar, or attending an event for a hobby you both love.

LEO: SURPRISING THEM

You know your partner best, but Leo is often a sign that appreciates gifts (and gifting) as a major part of their love language. They love any kind of surprise, whether it's a sweet treat after a long day, a bouquet of flowers, a heartfelt card, or even a more significant, personalized gift. You don't have to spend any money to make Leo happy—you just need to show them that you were thinking about them. These types of surprises give them something that makes them feel cared about and keeps them on their toes, making things feel exciting in between your everyday lives.

VIRGO: PLANNING RECURRING DATE NIGHTS

A great way to show Virgo you care is by taking the time to schedule out your date nights in advance. To keep things exciting without disrupting their busy schedule, set a specific day or time each week to do something together. Then, take over the planning with something new each week. Whether you want a casual movie night, a fancy night out on the town, or a full-day adventure, you'll both be setting aside time in your schedules to keep your relationship interesting.

SCORPIO: TEST OUT COUPLES' QUESTIONS

Scorpio sometimes has a hard time opening up, but they'll respond well to genuine care and curiosity from you. You might look into questions that can help the two of you learn more about each other and your relationship goals. Think about questionnaires like the NYT's 32 Questions to Fall in Love or couple's games that focus on asking and answering a deck of questions. Though this might feel a little cheesy to the two of you at first, they do genuinely open up the opportunity for you to both get to know each other more in a way that simply wouldn't come up naturally in conversation. Even if you've been together for a while, these kinds of questions often bring up answers that you won't have heard before.

SAGITTARIUS: COUPLES' GETAWAYS OR DAY TRIPS

For Sagittarius, a great way to bond and keep things interesting is by getting away for a while. They might be interested in an overnight camping trip or an easy day hike—maybe they'll want to take a well-planned yearly vacation with you, a road trip to a neighboring city, or just spend an afternoon at the beach. This gives them something to look forward to when things are feeling monotonous (a normal part of any relationship) and helps mix things up for Sagittarius in a way that they're bound to appreciate. Plus, these kinds of activities will help bond the two of you together.

CAPRICORN: HAVE FOCUSED DATE NIGHTS

Capricorn loves setting goals. They want to make sure they're on target for everything they want in life. Believe it or not, you can set up relationship goals and targets, too. Creating a date night to chat with Capricorn about new goals or ideas you have for the two of you as a couple—adding more spontaneous dates, trying an activity together, communicating in a new way—will keep things exciting in a way that Capricorn can easily understand. This kind of communication is super important to Capricorn and helps them learn to keep things interesting without overwhelming them or making them anxious.

AQUARIUS: FOCUS ON THEIR INTERESTS

Aquarius probably enjoys talking to you about their work and their passions. Even after you've gotten to know them entirely, they're probably still itching to talk to you about the things they like—even if they're things you already know by this point! Discussing the day-to-day of their passions, hobbies, and how their work is going is super important to Aquarius. To keep things exciting, try to learn something new about their work or ask a specific question about their hobby each day. In the long term, see if you can invest in their work in other ways—by asking to join in on a hobby night or read something about their interests.

PISCES: TRY A NEW CREATIVE HOBBY

Pisces can get bored easily—they always want to be working on something or creating something. They're an extremely creative type, so focusing on creative activities as a couple can be a good way to spark their interest. The key with Pisces is not just to switch things up with couples activities, but also to do something that the two of you haven't done together every so often. You might want to dive in headfirst by seeking out something that both of you are genuinely bad at, or just look for creative interests that neither of you have tried out. You might also look for Pisces to teach you something that they're good at, or vice versa. This gives you both the opportunity to look at an activity you've done before in a new light.

HERE'S THE ROMANCE MOVIE TROPE YOU'D FALL FOR, BASED ON YOUR ZODIAC SIGN

ARIES: SECRET IDENTITY

You're a sign that probably looks for more than just romance in a romance movie. This means that your favorite trope is one that involves drama and hidden secrets. To you, the idea of a secret identity romance is extra exciting. It usually involves a main character or love interest who is hiding their identity from the other person—whether they're secretly a billionaire, someone super famous, an online celebrity, or even a person from their past that they no longer recognize. This gives plenty of room for drama, fun, and a long road to real romance.

TAURUS: CHILDHOOD SWEETHEARTS

You're big on routine and can often be nostalgic at times, Taurus. There's nothing cuter than seeing an on-screen couple who keeps coming back to each other at different points in their lives. For you, someone who knows the ins and outs of your personality is important; you like seeing the idea of a couple who has literally known each other for every single stage of their lives.

GEMINI: FIRST LOVE (AND SECOND CHANCE LOVERS)

You're a little bit nostalgic, and with your large social circle, the trope of falling for someone from your past might be appealing to you. First love tropes usually involve a portion of the film dedicated to someone's first crush, first relationship, or first short romance. But you tend to go for the movies that don't just move on from the first love, but move back to the first love later. A main character gets the opportunity to fall in love with their first love all over again, proving that true soulmates really do exist. You're a sucker for a sweet, fun, and sometimes bittersweet trope—depending on your mood, you can find all three in a first love or second chance romance.

CANCER: FRIENDS TO LOVERS

Is there any surprise that you're a big fan of friends to lovers? You enjoy classic, innocent romance tropes—you're big on sweet and heartwarming stories through and through. You also don't tend to enjoy the dramatic will-they won't-they plot line that often comes with romance movies. To you, the couple that gently transitions from best friends to partners is always the most swoon-worthy romance.

LEO: THE LOVE TRIANGLE

A lot of people hate love triangles. But for someone who loves attention and drama, there's probably nothing you enjoy more than watching all the drama of a main character who has two love interests to choose from. You probably have a good methodology for figuring out who the main character is going to end up with—but you still love every second of the romance mystery.

VIRGO: PRETENDING TO DATE

You're not normally a person who enjoys drama, but you can definitely get a kick out of romances that involve secret relationships. The dating-not-dating trope follows a couple who has to pretend to date for one reason or another…but actually ends up falling in love. Usually there are plenty of side love interests and funny ways the ruse almost comes to light—and your attention to detail means you'll enjoy trying to pick up on all the ways the pretend relationship is about to be revealed…Until they actually start dating, of course.

LIBRA: FORBIDDEN LOVE

Hear this one out, Libra! In your daily life, you're interested in fairness and doing what's right. But when you need to unwind, your guilty pleasure might just be the forbidden love trope. It's fun trying to watch two people come together when circumstances say otherwise. You like the idea of a love that can defy all odds. For you, you might even find a sweet sense of justice in forbidden loves where a couple is able to unite two families, places, or friend groups through the sheer power of romance.

SCORPIO: ENEMIES TO LOVERS

Your sign is always going to fall for the classic enemies to lovers trope. Not only are you a big fan of these dramatic storylines, your very own sign enjoys getting to know someone slowly. As someone who has a hard time trusting people, it's romantic for you to think about a relationship that goes from hate to love as two people get to know each other over a long period of time.

SAGITTARIUS: SOULMATES OR DESTINED LOVERS

You're kind of a secret romantic at heart, Sagittarius! You really love the idea of someone who comes to you and seems to know everything about you; a soulmate who is made for you and only you. That's why you love the soulmate romance trope. Not only are they often involved in a grand adventure or larger plot, there's also the comfort of watching an on-screen romance that believes in complete, true love.

CAPRICORN: MEET-CUTES

You're a big planner, Capricorn, but you love to enjoy a romance trope that's entirely coincidental. It's a nice idea that the perfect person can fall right into your lap, and you're a sucker for trope-y meet-cutes in romance movies. Whether it's two people colliding with each other in a hallway and dropping all their papers or the future couple that reaches for the same book in a library, you're a sucker for the plot that shows two people really can stumble across each other at the right time.

AQUARIUS: SUPERNATURAL ROMANCE

You're a sucker for romance tropes that involve all the classic supernatural beings—vampires, elves, maybe even werewolves. You're interested in the quirky and in the unique; a lot of these films explore quirky traits by displaying them in characters that aren't entirely human. This makes for an interesting romance to you, and you might even like watching the idea of a regular human getting to fall in love with the supernatural.

PISCES: FAIRYTALES

You're a big fan of the fairytale romance, Pisces. You want a love-at-first-sight story that has a happy ending. You love traditional fairytales that feature timeless, classic romance stories that everyone knows. You don't mind if things are predictable or even a little sappy—for you, that's the best kind of romance.

LOOK OUT FOR THESE TAROT CARDS IF YOU'RE FALLING IN LOVE

THE LOVERS

The name tells all with this tarot card. If you're falling in love, you're much more likely to see the Lovers appear. This card signifies your hopes and dreams when it comes to romance. If you're falling in love with someone who is a healthy match for you, you're likely to want a stable future with them—and the Lovers represent that desire. They're all about achieving true romance and forming a complete relationship with someone else.

FOUR OF WANDS

The Four of Wands is a positive reading for those in relationships and those who are still looking for love. If you've fallen in love with someone you're already in a relationship with, the Four of Wands may be telling you that you are both truly in love with each other in a healthy way; that loyalty, security, and trust exist between the two of you. If you're single and falling in love with someone new, the Four of Wands signifies that there's potential for you on the horizon, so keep your heart open when it comes to romance!

KNIGHT OF CUPS

The Knight of Cups often appears when you have a potential partner awaiting you. The Knight himself plays the role of the person courting you in a reading; someone has fallen for you, and the ball might just be in your court. The Knight of Cups often appears when new romance is budding between you and someone else or when you're starting to think about making the first move yourself. The Knight of Cups often signifies bravery, adventure, and new beginnings—you might see this card when you're thinking about beginning a new romance or want to take a new step in your relationship.

THESE ZODIAC DUOS ARE PERFECT SOULMATES— BUT THERE'S ONE RELATIONSHIP STRUGGLE THEY NEED TO LOOK OUT FOR

GEMINI & AQUARIUS

These two signs are often touted as perfect soulmates, with an equal interest in intellectual discussion, exciting hobbies, and forward thinking. But there is a roadblock that this couple will need to keep an eye on: communication. Though there's nothing these two partners love more than open dialogue, they do have slightly different communication styles that may cause miscommunication or misunderstandings throughout the relationship.

Gemini tends to be a social sign who doesn't mind talking things out. When they sense something is off balance, they want to address it quickly. They might want to check in with their partner frequently and talk to them all the time—whether that's about serious topics or just fun things that are on their mind. To Gemini, sharing is caring!

For Aquarius, however, though they love Gemini's endless conversation during certain periods, they also tend to withdraw from all of their relationships for short periods of time. On occasion, Aquarius might get wrapped up in their work (or just feel highly introverted) and need time to recharge their social battery. This, unfortunately, also pertains to their partners, which can leave their partner confused and upset at being suddenly withdrawn from.

While Aquarius wants time to work, Gemini might think that something is seriously wrong in the relationship. Gemini will want to address this distance by talking with Aquarius, which will cause Aquarius to isolate even further, stirring up uncertainty and emotional dissonance between the two. To address this, Gemini and Aquarius just need to be mindful of each other's communication styles—Gemini shouldn't worry when Aquarius needs time to themselves, and Aquarius should be careful to reassure Gemini that everything is okay before going AWOL.

TAURUS & CANCER

This caring duo is recognized as an easy match for both signs. One sign of trouble the two might run into is Cancer's people-pleasing tendencies coupled with Taurus's stubbornness. It's too easy for Taurus to insist on something during a disagreement or relationship issue, and Cancer can't help but naturally feel inclined to agree.

To further this issue, Taurus often lashes out in a rage and feels upset at everything (and everyone) while they're experiencing a personal problem or just a bad day. Cancer, a nurturing sign, might willingly take the brunt of this anger—which can create burnout or resentment for Cancer later on.

To combat this, Taurus and Cancer will need to work out ways they can resolve disagreements without either of the two sacrificing their personal wellbeing. Taurus needs to find an emotional outlet that they can go to before they lash out at Cancer, and Cancer needs to help Taurus by setting boundaries when they need to have an emotional discussion. The two may also benefit from writing down thoughts they want to share with each other so that both signs have the chance to speak when they're not feeling emotionally vulnerable.

Additionally, Taurus and Cancer will need to recognize the ways they might interact unhealthily—with Cancer wanting to take on the emotional work for Taurus and Taurus being overly stubborn—to avoid them in the future. This can help the duo understand when they might need to adjust how they communicate or take a break from heated discussion.

VIRGO & CAPRICORN

This practical couple is loyal in love and communicates effectively. They're basically a lovable power duo, and they're likely to find each other an ideal match. The relationship issue they're most likely to experience, however, is being prone to overthinking.

Virgo is a sign who tends to overanalyze small details—especially when they're anxious about something. If they're nervous about something in the relationship or want to reassure themselves, they might look too hard into minor details—which will undoubtedly end with them only feeling more anxious or upset. Capricorn, on the other hand, is a chronic overthinker. It comes from them wanting to feel prepared for anything and ends with them feeling anxious about all the possibilities that they might be faced with.

The most effective way for these two signs to resolve their overthinking is to communicate as quickly as possible and recognize when they might be seeking reassurance (and what might be triggering them). If Virgo starts overthinking little details, they may want to figure out what the root cause is and try to address it, either with Capricorn or on their own time. When Capricorn wants to address a million tiny possibilities with Virgo, they should do the same thing—find the major root of the issue and decide whether they can resolve it introspectively or by talking with the other sign.

FEELING LUCKY IN LOVE? HERE'S YOUR SIGN IT'S GOING TO WORK OUT (ZODIAC EDITION)

ARIES

Aries, you'll know a relationship is going to work out when you and your partner start planning long-term goals together. There's nothing you love more than success (and maybe a little friendly competition), so it's a good sign for you when your partner matches your values and wants to seriously plan out your future together.

TAURUS

When a relationship is going strong for you, you'll be able to rely on them emotionally—and vice versa. You tend to have a set number of people that you look to for comfort and care, so when your partner becomes one of those people, you should know that you've found someone you can truly rely on long-term.

GEMINI

If your partner shows genuine interest in your hobbies, you might have just gotten your dream romance, Gemini. That's not to say that your partner has to come fully equipped with the exact same roster of hobbies you do—and that's probably not even something you'd want, seeing as your interests are constantly changing. But when you've found someone that gets excited by the things you're interested in (and is willing to try them with you…or just listen to you ramble), you know you've found your true match.

CANCER

You sometimes struggle to find people that will genuinely listen to you, Cancer. As a sign that everyone feels they're able to rely on, you're familiar with caring for those around you. When you've found that rare person that doesn't interrupt and loves to listen to you speak your mind, you'll know you've found a proper soulmate.

LEO

You'll know things are going to work out with someone when you no longer have to put up a front around them. You're a generous sign and you also love to (politely) flaunt your accomplishments and achievements. As an optimistic, sunny sign, you also may feel like you just can't have a bad day. When you feel safe enough to express unhappiness around your partner (and not feel like a failure for doing so), you'll know you might have found 'the one'.

VIRGO

The right relationship for you will mean your partner shows their love for you through their thoughtfulness, Virgo. If you're looking for a sign that it's going to work out, you should look for meaningful attempts from your partner to show that you're always on their mind. Whether they make an effort to remember your favorite color or flower or just want to pick up a little treat for you when you're feeling down, these small moments can really hit you with the realization that you're falling in love.

LIBRA

If you're looking for a sign things are going to work out, just look for someone you feel comfortable disagreeing with. Once you've hit this point, Libra, it means you're seriously emotionally connected with your partner and feel safe around them. It's the best sign for you that you're with the right person.

SCORPIO

One way to know that your relationship is going to work out is if your partner seems to be strangely intuitive about you…and vice versa. You take a while to open up to someone, so if you're looking for a sign that you're with your soulmate, you might look for a partner who is in-tune with what you're feeling. They don't need to predict everything about you, but for you, a partner who knows when you want to leave a party and go home or understands when you need your space is important. This doesn't mean they'll be telepathic—just that they know your preferences as well as you do.

SAGITTARIUS

When a relationship is going to work out, you won't worry about independence or freedom anymore. You're someone who doesn't really enjoy being tied down, so you might struggle to work a job or sign a lease that's going to keep you in one place for a while. To feel secure, you need to know you have an out. When you reach a point with your partner where you don't want to run away (or you do want to run away—with them), you'll know you've met your ideal match.

CAPRICORN

You'll know you're with your perfect partner when you feel that you can securely plan your future with them. You're someone who likes to be prepared for every possibility, having contingency plan after contingency plan for every little life detail. When you start planning your serious goals with your partner—without even a second thought—you'll know your subconscious is comfortable about getting serious with them.

AQUARIUS

When you find yourself with someone who challenges your ideas, you've met your match. A good sign for you to look out for is a person who you can have open discussions with about the things you're interested in. They won't be afraid to contribute to your work projects or just pose philosophical questions for you to think on.

PISCES

A good sign your relationship is going to work out is when they communicate openly and honestly with you—and listen to your needs, too. You look for partners that will tell you exactly what they're feeling and why (and will work with you to fix any relationship issues that arise). Having this kind of open dialogue is important to you—and when it's present in your relationship, it's a good sign things will work out.

THESE 4 ZODIAC SIGNS CAN'T DO CASUAL RELATIONSHIPS

TAURUS

If you know Taurus at all, you know that they prefer comfort and stability over everything else. For them, a relationship can sometimes be a source of anxiety even when it's more serious; throwing them into a casual relationship makes them on edge, all the time. Taurus needs to know if they're able to rely on their partner for security and comfort. A casual relationship just doesn't fulfill this need for Taurus, so they either find themselves clinging to something casual in the hopes that it will turn serious or just totally shutting their casual date out. If you want to romance Taurus, you should be prepared for a commitment.

SCORPIO

Scorpio is an intense character, and they usually look for a passionate connection in their romantic relationships. They want a relationship that's deep and meaningful. In a casual relationship, they just won't find that. Scorpio's walls only really come down once they feel they can completely trust and rely on their partner, which won't usually happen for them in a casual relationship. This can make them feel closed off to casual partners, denying Scorpio the emotional experience they truly want in a relationship. For many Scorpios, dating no one is better than dating casually.

CANCER

It's probably no surprise that Cancer, a sign that values sentimentality and close connections with loved ones, isn't good at casual relationships. They're the kind of sign who would get into a casual relationship and quickly develop serious feelings, often leading to them getting hurt. They sometimes have trouble setting boundaries and saying no to people, especially those they admire. But Cancer often struggles to deal with the idea of forming a connection with someone that never really goes anywhere.

LIBRA

Libra is a mediator at heart, which means they like to know exactly what's going on at all times. They're not comfortable with ambiguity; they want things to be clear right away. Casual relationships often come with a sense of uncertainty that Libra just doesn't appreciate; Libra tends to prefer relationships that are definitive. They want the long-term stability and emotional security that comes, for Libra, only when they make a more serious commitment. Otherwise, they may struggle to express themselves and their needs—if they feel that they're risking the entire relationship every time they speak up for themselves, it will never work out. This is why Libra isn't usually very good with keeping things casual.

THESE ZODIAC SIGNS ARE UNLIKELY SOULMATES

LIBRA & SCORPIO

Although Libra and Scorpio's personalities contrast each other, these two signs can make a surprisingly strong pairing depending on the individuals. Libra and Scorpio are basically a power couple; Libra is socially graceful and strong-willed, while Scorpio is charismatic and easy to like. This makes an unusual but complementary pairing. As all Libras would undoubtedly enjoy, a Scorpio and Libra pairing can be extraordinarily balanced.

The struggle for this pairing comes with their communication. In order for Scorpio and Libra to find success, Scorpio will need to make room for Libra to comfortably address their concerns, while Libra will need to work on standing up for themselves when they need to. Scorpio needs to focus on listening to Libra and making sure they feel on equal footing in their relationship; Libra will need to give Scorpio time to open up to them.

TAURUS & AQUARIUS

Taurus and Aquarius have opposing personalities in some ways, but they may be more able to support each other than most people think. Aquarius is a dedicated innovator, always hard at work, while Taurus prefers creature comforts and can be stubborn in their ways. This leaves room for these two signs to draw the best out of each other; Aquarius can help Taurus step out of their comfort zone and find new passions, while Taurus is a comfortable, stable person for Aquarius to care for.

The biggest clash for this pairing comes with Taurus's love for tradition and Aquarius's love of new innovations. In order for this couple to be successful, they'll need to find a way to compromise on Taurus's need for routine traditions while also satisfying Aquarius's drive towards the new and futuristic. Even though both sides of the couple can be relatively stubborn, this is an item that these two signs will likely be able to compromise on.

GEMINI & CAPRICORN

This zodiac pairing is surprisingly similar in many ways. Both Gemini and Capricorn are dedicated to their passions—Gemini loves to stay just as busy as Capricorn does, and they're both signs who enjoy intellectual conversation. Capricorn's discipline and Gemini's love of varied activities means neither sign will mind when the other is busy with work. Capricorn's relationship strength comes in their penchant for discipline, which will help them with long-term goals, while Gemini is a fast and furious pursuer of what they're interested in.

The biggest issue for this couple is if they can't agree on any mutual desires. Gemini often has many things they want, all of which change quickly; Capricorn tends to be more dedicated to a single goal at a time. When these things align, all will be well with this couple. But the two will need to learn to compromise, so that Capricorn can be satisfied with their accomplishments and Gemini will have enough variety to stimulate their curiosity.

4 ZODIAC SIGNS WHO LOVE ROMANTIC SURPRISES

PISCES

Pisces is a romantic at heart, and they're a dreamer, too—they've probably already thought of a million different romantic surprises they'd enjoy. They're a sign who doesn't mind spontaneity, especially when it comes as a gesture of love from a person they care about. Pisces is also a naturally creative sign, so don't be afraid to think outside the box when it comes to surprises for them. With Pisces, it's important to keep in mind that they're a caring and sentimental sign; choosing a surprise that has special meaning for your relationship or to Pisces specifically will always be the way to go. Whether you remember something they love or want to recreate a moment meaningful to the two of you, you can't go wrong with a tailored romantic surprise for Pisces.

LEO

Leo is big on grand gestures of love—so what better way to show your appreciation than by surprising them? As a creative with a flair for the dramatic, Leo typically loves being surprised, especially when it comes to romantic relationships. They like receiving a lot of attention and will want to know you care about them; surprising them with something is a good way to reassure them you like them. As a sign who's into theatrics and luxury, a surprise is a great way to bring a random gift or special outing for Leo to the next level.

SAGITTARIUS

Sagittarius thrives on spontaneity. Usually, they're the ones who are thinking out of the box when it comes to where to go or what to do; sometimes, Sagittarius can even surprise themselves with a random plan they come up with on the fly. Taking initiative and planning an unexpected surprise for Sagittarius can be a fun way to engage them—and you don't have to plan any major trips for them to be excited about what you have planned. A quick drive, hike, or random gift will be enough to catch them off guard—just know that they'll probably want to return the favor at some point.

CANCER

Cancer is a sentimental sign. They love a good nostalgic moment, and you'll often find them reminiscing over memories with those they care about. Surprising Cancer in a way that involves their sentimental side is the way to go. You could present them with a meaningful gift—like a photo album or handwritten letter—or take them someplace you haven't been before to create new memories for them to look back on. Just know that Cancer doesn't always like being caught off guard, so smaller surprises are usually better to start with if you don't know them that well. A sentimental and sweet surprise will always win Cancer over, though.

THESE TAROT CARDS COULD MEAN YOU'VE FOUND TRUE LOVE

THE LOVERS

You can probably already guess by its name that The Lovers card means good news in all things romance. It's all about the strong bond between lovers, pure love, and genuine connection. The Lovers covers everything authentic and true—it's basically the tarot's way of saying you might have found your soulmate.

TWO OF CUPS

The Two of Cups is all about unity between two things. If you're wondering about your romantic life, the Two of Cups is a great card to receive; it can symbolize the partnership between two people, making it a strong indicator of true love. Two of Cups means that you might be developing a new relationship with someone who is your perfect match or that you're solidifying a bond between you and the one you love. It's also often recognized as a twin flame card.

FOUR OF WANDS

Especially if you have a romance-related query for the deck, receiving the Four of Wands could be good news for your romantic life. Four of Wands indicates a time of joy and happiness. It's a celebratory card that shows things are going well for you or are about to get even better. In terms of love, it means that you and your partner are about to experience true bliss together. You have things to celebrate in your partnership together and have found happiness and peace with one another.

ACE OF CUPS

If you're in a new relationship with someone, the Ace of Cups is the perfect card to receive. It usually signifies new beginnings and new possibilities. When it comes to your love life, it means that you've found or are about to find someone who you can truly connect with and find deep love with. For those in established relationships, the Ace of Cups can represent joyful romantic periods and intimacy.

4 ZODIAC SIGNS WHO ARE LETTING RELATIONSHIP ANXIETY SABOTAGE THEM

LIBRA

Libra, your sign naturally comes with a lot of social magnetism and grace. However, you tend to fear the worst when it comes to relationships. Your tendency to avoid conflicts means that you're often scared of your partner's reaction when raising any issues you're experiencing in your relationship. Your sign would rather sometimes put up with small problems that are easily changeable out of the unrealistic fear that your partner will leave you at the drop of a hat. In the end, this only builds resentment and prevents you from communicating clearly with your partner.

VIRGO

Virgo, your sign is known for noticing the little things. This also means that you tend to overthink small details. When you're feeling anxious, any action your partner takes is subject to analysis. Things that your partner does without even thinking about could send you spiraling—and you may accidentally draw back from your partner (in their mind, for no apparent reason) over something you're worried about. This isolates you from your partner and leaves the two of you feeling disconnected, making your worries feel even more realistic.

SCORPIO

Scorpio, once you show your true self to someone, you fear them leaving you in the dust. This makes you struggle to fully trust your partner and could leave you feeling like you're never really safe letting your guard down. Whether you never fully open up to your partner or just fall into anxious spirals as soon as you feel like you trust them, it can be difficult for you to let go of the need for control and constant moderation in your relationships.

CANCER

Cancer, as a sensitive sign, you tend to worry about how your partner perceives you. You're constantly stressed out by what you're perceiving they're saying or thinking about you, even if you're way off base. Though you're great at emotional perception, your anxiety can really throw off your intuition—for a sign who's used to trusting their emotional capabilities, this can be scary! You might feel like you have no choice but to rely on your intuition when it comes to your romantic relationships, even if it's out of whack thanks to your anxious thoughts. This does nothing but cause you to spiral out even more and create a huge emotional gap between you and your partner.

IF YOU MET YOUR SOULMATE, THESE TAROT CARDS WILL APPEAR

THE LOVERS

Of course the Lovers are going to be the brightest sign when it comes to romantic tarot cards. The Lovers come together when your relationship is in alignment; they signify that you may have found someone who meets your values, who you can stand by authentically and love deeply. The Lovers represent the ideal relationship. This may signify a future potential for the both of you, or it could signal that you have reached true bliss if you've been in a relationship for a long time.

TWO OF CUPS

The Two of Cups is all about partnership. Your emotional cups are literally being filled by each other; you are deeply bonded with your partner and your energies are aligned with one another. The Two of Cups is often considered to be a soulmate card by many tarot readers; if you and your partner pull this card frequently, it could be a good sign for the both of you.

THE EMPRESS

The Empress is another positive card to receive if you're wondering whether you've found your soulmate. The Empress is a nurturer, and she's often said to signify true and healthy love. The Empress brings about secure, deep romance; love that is built on connection and partnership that is long-lasting. If you're in a healthy and stable relationship, the Empress could be signifying that your relationship's security is a positive for the both of you.

YOUR PARTNER'S BIRTH CARD

You might see your partner's birth card pop up frequently if the two of you are meant to be. You may not recognize it at first, but be on the lookout for it to appear during certain situations. It could come at times when you need reassurance, at meaningful points in your relationship, or when you and your partner are working together to resolve a relationship issue.

THESE ZODIAC SIGNS ARE MOST LIKELY TO MEET THEIR SOULMATE IN THE WINTER

SAGITTARIUS

Though you're an autumnal zodiac sign, your sign's season often covers both the end of fall and the beginning of winter. Many times, Sagittarius season will include the Winter Solstice. This makes you likely to find love in the middle of the coldest months of the year—but it's not just because you're at your most charming, confident, and optimistic (though that certainly helps).

As an adventurous, freedom-loving sign, you tend to feel more alive than most in the winter months. You don't want to go into hibernation—you take the colder weather as a sign to change up your routine and enjoy the outside world for a while. But the darkest days of the year are also when you start to realize that you might enjoy your adventures a little more if you had someone to go on them with. Your sign is highly independent and rarely lonely, so summer tends to be where you grow the most personally, whereas winter is where you flourish socially.

This leaves you to find romance in the winter. You're most likely to fall in love, start a long-term relationship, and—yes—find your soulmate in the cold months. You secretly love a good holiday date and dream of a simple walk beneath some twinkling lights.

PISCES

You're a hopeless romantic, Pisces—you've heard it before. Winter is your season, with your sign coming in at the very end of the coldest months to wrap up the season. But that doesn't mean winter isn't your time to find true love. It's your romantic nature that gets you there—yes, summer picnics are nice and all, but you harbor a true admiration for adorable holiday movies and cozy winter dates.

Winter tends to be a time where you can withdraw inward, reflect, and dream a little. But these dreams also inspire you to hope for romance. So, by the time Pisces season rolls around, you feel ready to start dating—or make your relationship much more serious. This means that you're likely to meet (or start a serious relationship with) your soulmate during the winter, though it will often be the last part of winter in which you do so.

CAPRICORN

You're goal-focused, Capricorn. You can't deny that the start of winter is a good time for you—during Capricorn season, your determination and disciplined nature truly shine. Though you may or may not feel a little more romantic during the winter—despite your stoic exterior—the winter months is where your personality truly starts to shine through. This attracts other people who admire you, leading you to find your soulmate (even if by accident).

If you've been working hard at your career, celebrating your successes within your social circle, or just taking the winter as an opportunity to invest more in your hobbies, you're likely to attract someone's romantic attention. All of these things are truly you, Capricorn—they showcase your hopes, your goals, your dreams, your values, and your personality. That's why you're most likely to meet your soulmate during winter; because they see you for who you are, and they love you for it.

WEALTH & FINANCES

Everything you ever wanted to know about making money and your financial future.

IF YOUR ZODIAC SIGN MADE THIS LIST, YOU NEED TO LEARN HOW TO MANAGE YOUR FINANCES

GEMINI

The sign of the twin sometimes comes in handy and sometimes doesn't when it comes to your sign, Gemini. That's the issue with having a dual nature—one day, you're saving judiciously for your future, the next, you're blowing it all on a passion project or new hobby. Your curiosity and love of new projects means that you might want to invest a lot of money into a new hobby that won't interest you for long, even as you also have big financial goals for your future. The best thing you can do for yourself is bridge the gap between your two sides by giving yourself enough spending money to satisfy your hobbies wherever possible while still saving some cash for later.

PISCES

When it comes to finances, you tend to dream big and ignore reality. You dedicate your life to your passions—a noble pursuit for sure—but often don't worry about future financial goals in the process. This means that you need to get better at budgeting, Pisces. It's a trait of your sign to want to live in the moment—but that doesn't mean you can't have the best of both worlds once you get better at walking the line between making your dreams come true and being realistic.

SAGITTARIUS

You dedicate much of your time to adventuring—even if your finances say otherwise. When it comes to managing various aspects of your life, you often have so much going on that your finances come last. Even though your sign does attract new money fairly well, it doesn't always stick around—and if it does, you don't know why or even where it is. You need to prioritize your finances and spend dedicated time getting your budget in order each month—or maybe even each week. Tracking your spending and making more of an effort to understand where your money is going can help you feel more on top of your finances (and maybe even show you some places you have a little extra room to spend).

THESE THREE ZODIAC SIGNS ARE PROVEN TO BE THE WEALTHIEST

Ever wondered whether astrology relates to the richest people in the world? After Forbes' list of 300 wealthiest billionaires was analyzed, it was found that there were some common trends when it came to the zodiac signs of the richest people alive. Here are the three zodiac signs most common amongst billionaires.

LIBRA

With Libra's charm, grace, and social skills, it's no surprise that they make up 12% of the world's billionaires. This puts them at the top of the list for common signs amongst the 300 richest people. Libra has a unique combination of determination, likeableness, and realism to achieve their goals. Libra loves the finer things in life and has an eye for aesthetics, which can sometimes make them susceptible to spending. But generally, they tend to manage their money well, which explains much of the financial prowess that surrounds their sign.

PISCES

Making up 11% of the world's billionaires, Pisces ranks second on the list. Surprisingly, Pisces isn't always known to be good with money—they can be forgetful and unrealistic, which could cause struggles with budgeting. But once the sign has this under control, they have the power to be extremely successful. Plus, Pisces tends to dream the biggest out of all the zodiac signs, and they have uniquely artistic visions and creative energies. It's not surprising that many Pisces have likely struck figurative gold, making vast amounts of fame and fortune off their creative ventures—whether that's selling artwork, making music, or launching a business.

TAURUS

Taurus is third on the list when it comes to the world's billionaires, making up 10% of them. Taurus is known for being able to manage money. They're grounded, enjoy coziness and basic creature comforts over extreme luxury, and track their spending well. They're also generally a risk-averse sign. They follow a stable, consistent routine, which keeps them on track with their goals and makes them professionally successful. All of these factors could contribute to the financial success of this sign.

THESE 4 ZODIAC SIGNS ARE OBSESSED WITH MAKING MONEY

ARIES

You're a competitive type who's well suited for jobs that involve a lot of challenge, leadership, and even high-stress scenarios. Where most people would burn out, you thrive. This also makes you a prime candidate for a high-paying career—which is a good thing, because your sign is likely to be fairly money-focused. That's not a bad thing. For one, you're competing with yourself to see how well you can perform and how much you can make. You're also focused on your goals and ambitions, so you likely want to have a lot of savings accounts or dedicate a certain amount of money to your hobbies. This makes you more controlling over your own money than most, but it usually turns out very well for you.

CAPRICORN

Your sign's obsession with money can vary from person to person. It's no surprise that Capricorns are on the top of the list for being good with finances. You're organized, you're risk-averse, and you set strict goals for yourself. Plus, you're disciplined with your spending. Your money obsession may not come from always needing to make more and more money, but rather from obsessively managing yourself and your goals to ensure you always know exactly where your money is going and where you could be saving more of it.

LEO

As a sign who loves luxury, you have to be on top of your budget. Your sign tends to be drawn towards things that are expensive—you just have fine taste, Leo. But your dedication towards your aesthetic preferences are actually supported by your budget. As a generous person, you need to have the means to support yourself and show appreciation for the ones you care about. You also tend to have gifting as a main love language for yourself, which may mean that you purchase frequent gifts for those you love. Fortunately, all of this is supported by a well-structured budget and a desire to always be making more money. You love to streamline your creative passions into money-making ventures and are always looking for another thing to add to your schedule that can increase your monthly budget.

VIRGO

You're organized, Virgo, and there's no doubt about that. It's that very same organization that lends itself to your money obsession. You reign tightly over your finances to ensure that everything is always in order. You might have a well-planned schedule of monthly purchases, enjoy hunting for the best deals on products you want to buy, and definitely have a schedule of yearly sales to shop at. You plan out large purchases well in advance and feel most secure when you have ample savings. This also makes you a little more obsessed than most when it comes to money and your earnings.

THIS IS THE WORST TAROT CARD TO RECEIVE FINANCIALLY

If you've been wondering about your financial future, tarot cards could give you some insight into the obstacles you'll face in the near future. Whether you've approached the deck with a specific question about your finances or are just waiting to see what they have in store generally, there tends to be one main card people think of when they think of bad news about money.

THE FIVE OF PENTACLES

The Five of Pentacles is difficult to see as anything but negative. Also known as the Five of Coins, the card features two people struggling through the snow outside of a church window. This card typically symbolizes financial hardship. It even has additional meanings that can also indicate financial strain—like illness or loss.

The Pentacles suit is most related to Earth signs astrologically. This makes the Pentacles suit most related to financials, whether good or bad. Many Pentacles cards represent good fortune and stability, and the Pentacles are often seen as the foundational cards of the Tarot deck.

Though the Five of Pentacles can be cause for concern, it doesn't always mean that you're going to go through long-term hardship. The Pentacles suit works to draw your attention towards something in your life that needs changing.

The Five of Pentacles could show up purely because you're worried about your finances or are feeling like you're under financial stress in your present moment. If you have financial problems from your past that you have not yet resolved, the Five of Pentacles could also be weighing on you heavily as a result of these. The card may also be warning you of upcoming financial hardships.

Five of Pentacles is also seen by some as a card that encourages the querent to ask for help. Though it often symbolizes hardship and struggle, many readers believe that the card is simply a sign that the querent needs assistance from others.

Of course, if you happen to get the Five of Pentacles reversed, it's likely a sign that positive change is coming to you financially. If you've been going through a tough period regarding your finances, things might be about to change for you. Especially if you've been noticing long-term financial decisions or commitments that have been weighing you down, the Five of Pentacles could symbolize an end to these—such as paying off a debt.

Receiving the upright Five of Pentacles doesn't necessarily mean that everything in your life is about to go downhill. You may receive some negative financial news or go through a period of struggle. But the card may also be warning you that it's time to pay attention to your financial life and ask for help from those you trust.

TAROT CARDS THAT SIGNAL A MILLIONAIRE'S PATH

TEN OF PENTACLES

If there's money involved, the Ten of Pentacles is the card you want to see. It's the quintessential representation of wealth. If you're searching for stability when it comes to your finances, then pulling the Ten of Pentacles is your sign.

The Ten of Pentacles is especially revered when it comes to financial success because it represents long-term financial growth and wealth. The Ten of Pentacles appears when your financial success will stay with you rather than be fleeting. When you grow your savings, make wise financial decisions, and work towards your financial goals over time, the Ten of Pentacles approves—and that's when it's most likely to appear to commend you on your efforts and remind you that a lifetime of wealth, joy, and abundance is on its way to you.

THE SUN

The Sun is all about success and happiness. If you are completing a financial reading or asking for financial advice, the Sun is the card you want to pull. It can indicate that you have already manifested or achieved wealth in some way; but it can also appear as a symbol of future prosperity. It guides you to continue working towards your goals and achieving what you hope for.

The Sun often represents good fortune, though it can do so in many more ways than just financial. This is why you should look out for the Sun when asking money-related questions or searching for financial guidance specifically, as it can have varied meanings that may apply to your life in multiple ways.

KING OF PENTACLES

The King of Pentacles is another great tarot card to look out for when it comes to financial success. He represents power and wealth, and is a likely indicator that financial fortune is coming your way.

Just keep in mind that the King of Pentacles often also deals with tradition and loyalty; this could mean that your savings journey is only just beginning if you haven't yet dedicated yourself to pursuing your financial goals. The King of Pentacles reminds you of how secure and prosperous you will someday be with dedication and trust.

ACE OF PENTACLES

The Ace of Pentacles is about a new journey. It encourages you to take action and embark on a journey you have been considering; to make the ideas you've been dreaming of a reality. It can also be an indicator that financial success is coming to you.

The Ace of Pentacles is more about predicting future success rather than commending you on a success you already have. If you're thinking about opening a savings account, starting a new budget, or setting a financial goal for yourself, for example, the Ace of Pentacles is a great sign that you're on track. It predicts financial success in your endeavors—as long as you take action towards your goals, of course.

THESE TAROT CARDS MEAN YOU'LL BE FINANCIALLY SUCCESSFUL

TEN OF PENTACLES

If there's money involved, the Ten of Pentacles is the card you want to see. It's the quintessential representation of wealth. If you're searching for stability when it comes to your finances, then pulling the Ten of Pentacles is your sign.

The Ten of Pentacles is especially revered when it comes to financial success because it represents long-term financial growth and wealth. The Ten of Pentacles appears when your financial success will stay with you rather than be fleeting. When you grow your savings, make wise financial decisions, and work towards your financial goals over time, the Ten of Pentacles approves—and that's when it's most likely to appear to commend you on your efforts and remind you that a lifetime of wealth, joy, and abundance is on its way to you.

THE SUN

The Sun is all about success and happiness. If you are completing a financial reading or asking for financial advice, the Sun is the card you want to pull. It can indicate that you have already manifested or achieved wealth in some way; but it can also appear as a symbol of future prosperity. It guides you to continue working towards your goals and achieving what you hope for.

The Sun often represents good fortune, though it can do so in many more ways than just financial. This is why you should look out for the Sun when asking money-related questions or searching for financial guidance specifically, as it can have varied meanings that may apply to your life in multiple ways.

KING OF PENTACLES

The King of Pentacles is another great tarot card to look out for when it comes to financial success. He represents power and wealth, and is a likely indicator that financial fortune is coming your way.

Just keep in mind that the King of Pentacles often also deals with tradition and loyalty; this could mean that your savings journey is only just beginning if you haven't yet dedicated yourself to pursuing your financial goals. The King of Pentacles reminds you of how secure and prosperous you will someday be with dedication and trust.

ACE OF PENTACLES

The Ace of Pentacles is about a new journey. It encourages you to take action and embark on a journey you have been considering; to make the ideas you've been dreaming of a reality. It can also be an indicator that financial success is coming to you.

The Ace of Pentacles is more about predicting future success rather than commending you on a success you already have. If you're thinking about opening a savings account, starting a new budget, or setting a financial goal for yourself, for example, the Ace of Pentacles is a great sign that you're on track. It predicts financial success in your endeavors—as long as you take action towards your goals, of course.

IF YOU'RE ONE OF THESE 3 ZODIAC SIGNS, YOU NEED TO LEARN HOW TO BUDGET

SAGITTARIUS

Sagittarius, since you're a spontaneous sign who enjoys a little bit of adventure every now and then (read: all the time), you need a budget that can keep up with your busy schedule. Your love of spontaneity means you may or may not have the funds for the next adventure you're dreaming up—and if you don't have a good idea of where your cash is going, you'll probably struggle to turn down the more expensive opportunities you come up with. Your sign would seriously benefit from a solid travel/adventure budget; once you have a goal in mind, you'd probably find it fairly easy to start saving up.

LEO

Leo, not only do you love luxury, you're also a highly generous sign. You care about others and want to share what you have with them—whether that's buying extravagant gifts for your loved ones' birthdays or grabbing a round for everyone at the bar. When you're looking to spend a lot (on yourself and others), you should also focus on creating a budget that can keep up. You'll need a good idea of how much you're regularly spending on gifts for yourself and gifts for other people, and you'll then need to adjust that amount accordingly. Try tracking your expenses for a while—and remember, generosity doesn't just come from material items.

ARIES

Because you're an impatient and impulsive individual, Aries, you also need to focus on curating a solid budget. The good news is that you're a prime candidate for big savings: once you have a goal for yourself, you basically can't help but achieve it. As long as you have a solid budget behind you, you'll be able to reign in impulsive spending. Since you're naturally competitive, you may want to have a competition with yourself each month to see how much you can save. You could even opt for a budget app that lets you challenge your friends or family with how much you can put away each month.

GEMINI

It's your love of variety that makes you in dire need of a budget, Gemini. You tend to hop around from one interest to another—great for your mind, but maybe not for your bank account. Focus on finding a budget that can help you track what you're spending on your hobbies. Once you're ready to cut down, you can determine when hobby-jumping is right for you or when you need to cut down on spending for a bit. For your curious mind, finding thriftier activities for you (and your friends) could also be a fun challenge.

BREAKUPS & HEALING

How to help yourself heal and recover from your past.

WHY YOU CAN'T LET GO, BASED ON YOUR ZODIAC SIGN

ARIES: YOU'RE TOO AMBITIOUS

Aries, your sign may struggle with something akin to the sunk cost fallacy. When you've been working on something for a long time—a friendship, a career—all you can think about is the energy and time you've put into it. You're a competitive sign, which means you hate giving up; especially on things you've had or wanted for a while. Even when something is no longer right for you, you don't want to spend your days wondering if you should have done more.

TAURUS: YOU'RE STUBBORN

Sign of the bull, it's no secret that you always like to get your way. When you want something you can't have, it feels like the best thing for you to do is lock down. You don't want to change your routine or let go of the things you cherish. In your mind, if you just hold on hard enough, nothing will ever have to ruin your stability and routine. But this isn't always the case, Taurus—and even if it was, all signs have to go through change; even the most stubborn one.

GEMINI: YOU WANT IT ALL AT ONCE

You're probably used to being told that you like to juggle things, Gemini. You're a flexible sign who always wants to be busy. You jump from project to project, so it may seem like you have an easy time letting go of things that don't interest you. But that's not necessarily true; when there's something you're interested in, even if it's not right for you, you can't help but fixate on it (along with all your other interests, of course). This makes it hard for you to let go of something your mind sees as 'fun' or 'interesting,' because your curiosity can never truly be satisfied.

CANCER: YOU'RE SENTIMENTAL

Your sign is known for being nostalgic and sentimental; you cherish your loved ones, your memories, and your sentimental objects. This makes it difficult for you to let go of something because you always want to hold on; whether this includes memories that have turned bittersweet, objects you don't need, or even relationships that have turned toxic. You always want to think about the good times, and sometimes your sentimentality can cloud reality; you see things through the lens of the past rather than understanding that they're not right for you anymore in the present.

LEO: YOU WANT THE ACHIEVEMENT

Whether you're looking for praise or another accolade to add to your shelf, you struggle to let go because you fear failure, Leo. This doesn't just apply to your professional life—it could be that rocky friendship you wanted to keep or the personal project you were hoping to show off to everyone. Especially once you've told others in your life about something meaningful to you, you struggle to let go of it—you don't like people thinking you're wrong or make bad decisions. That's not really the case here, though, Leo; things change, and so do people. You're allowed to switch things up when they're not right for you anymore; most people have to at some point.

LIBRA: YOU FEAR CONFLICT

If you have a project that's causing you to burn out or a relationship you just don't want to continue, you have a hard time telling anyone, Libra. Maybe you're letting work pile on because you just don't want to turn anyone down or maybe you're continuing relationships you've outgrown because you can't stand the thought of confrontation. When you absolutely have to let go of something, you tend to try your best at a 'slow fade'—and if it doesn't work, you often avoid letting go entirely just so that you don't have to enter a conflict with anyone.

VIRGO: YOU STRIVE FOR PERFECTION

To you, Virgo, letting go of something can feel like failure. For a sign who has an extensive to-do list and a track record of catching things nobody else can, it can feel like it goes against your very being to just…give up. Ask yourself, Virgo, is reassessing the same as giving up? Is letting go of something that no longer serves you the same as failure? For true perfection, you should strive to make your life as easy and pleasant for you as possible; this means accepting the fact that you can't achieve what isn't right for you.

SCORPIO: YOU NEED CONTROL

Your sign likes to be in control because it gives you reassurance, Scorpio. You struggle to let go of things when doing so is completely out of your control; you want to have the power in any given situation because it comforts you to know that things are in your hands. When that's taken away from you, you may feel like you want to hold onto something longer than you should in the hopes that you can regain some control over it. This doesn't usually work out as you hope it would, though,

Scorpio; ironically, you can find the most control by accepting that sometimes, you just don't have any.

SAGITTARIUS: YOU'RE OPTIMISTIC

Your optimism is a good thing, Sagittarius, let's be clear. But it's also an explanation for why you might struggle to let go sometimes. You want to see the best in people and you want to believe the best for yourself. If your career doesn't suit you anymore, you want to hope that you can adapt and that things will get better. If your relationships have turned toxic, you want to hang onto the past and assure yourself that things aren't as bad as they seem. Even though you value your freedom, this doesn't mean you don't get attached to people, places, and things; your disposition makes it hard for you to see that you really need to let go of something when you're in the moment.

CAPRICORN: YOU NEVER GIVE UP

Your sign is conditioned to meet (and beat) your goals no matter what, Capricorn. Giving up just isn't in your vocabulary, no matter how many new projects you have on your plate or how far away your desires may seem. Whether it's people, projects, or life goals, despite your sign's realism, you struggle to release things that no longer serve you. Rather than seeing that letting go is a method of growth, you see it as a sign of failure. That's not true, Capricorn; sometimes, you need to reevaluate what you really want.

AQUARIUS: YOU HAVE A VISION FOR THE FUTURE

You're a forward-thinker, Aquarius, which means that you struggle to let go of things you thought you'd have forever. Maybe you were busy planning the next several decades of your life in a particular job you never thought you'd stop liking. Maybe you thought you'd stick with the same circle of people forever. Maybe you never wanted to move out of where you're living now. You build the ideal world for yourself because it's what your sign wants to create; as a humanitarian, you're constantly imagining what could be for the world (and how to get there). When you do the same thing for yourself, though, you sometimes forget that variables can change on a whim, which makes it difficult for you to let go of things that aren't serving you anymore because you thought you needed them to stay the same forever.

PISCES: YOU WANT YOUR DREAMS TO WORK OUT

You've probably been told that you're a dreamer a million times, Pisces; it's the most striking trait of your sign. These dreams can help you understand yourself better; you know yourself well, are aware of your subconscious desires, and know what you want to achieve to be satisfied with yourself. But you sometimes struggle to pull these dreams into reality, especially since your sign loves to dream big. When something isn't right for you anymore, you struggle to differentiate between the dream where everything works out perfectly and the reality where you need to let go of a goal you wanted to achieve. These kinds of dreams can haunt you, Pisces, making you feel like you could have had it all if you just kept going; but, as intuitive as you are, not all dreams are meant to be real. Sometimes, you need to let go for your own sake.

EASY WAYS TO PROMOTE HEALING, BASED ON YOUR ZODIAC SIGN

ARIES

One easy way for your sign to help promote healing is to exercise—the harder the better. As someone who is naturally competitive (and as a strong fire sign), you're likely to find that physical activity helps you release your energy and let go of negative emotions you've been holding onto. Doing something challenging can help you get your confidence back and reel in your focus to help you process.

TAURUS

As an earth sign who appreciates small, comforting moments, immersing yourself in nature can be extremely healing. Walking or sitting in natural areas can help you think, process, and promote healing. Best of all, you may also find that it calms your body and nervous system, making it easier to focus or helping you feel less anxious.

GEMINI

For a sign who's always on the go, gratitude journaling can be a wonderful and easy way to promote healing in your life. Since your sign is usually busy with lots of different activities, gratitude journaling can help you appreciate every facet of your life—even the things you normally wouldn't stop to think about. This can help promote feelings of positivity, new energy, and create a healing mindset for you to benefit from throughout the day.

CANCER

The easiest way to help yourself heal is to receive affirming words or gentle physical touch from your loved ones. Whether you want to visit your family for a day, spend a night with your partner, or enjoy time with friends, doing so can help you heal significantly. You cherish time spent with those close to you and can often benefit from their advice and kindness. Allow the focus to be on you for a time.

LEO

Self-expression is everything to you, Leo. It's important for you to have a unique sense of style and passions that express your truest personality. A simple way you can promote healing is to get dressed up—whether it's for a fancy event or for absolutely nothing at all. This can help you not only find a straightforward activity that brings positivity to your day, but can also help you rediscover yourself and your identity if you've been feeling lost or unconfident lately. This can be a great marker for beginning the healing process and even help you continue to process your healing, too.

VIRGO

For you, Virgo, you might feel worse when your space is out of order. In fact, a messy space can make it difficult to focus on personal healing, because your mind perceives it as an extra (but often subconscious) burden you need to take care of. Just having a messy space can deplete your energy stores. On the other hand, the act of cleaning and organizing can be highly meditative, giving your brain the time and space to sort its thoughts and begin the healing process as you physically sort and organize your own space.

LIBRA

You can be a highly social sign, Libra, but also a sign who needs to set boundaries in order to avoid burning out. To promote healing, you may find the simple act of giving yourself alone time intensely healing. As a way of processing and promoting mental healing, you should give yourself as little as a few minutes each day to sit alone in silence with your thoughts. It's a good way to help you restore your energy, focus, and align your intentions.

SCORPIO

As a sign who's good at communicating with their subconscious and is likely to enjoy writing, journaling is a good way for you to promote healing, Scorpio. It allows you to write out your authentic emotions and feelings on a subject—even if you're not ready for other people to hear them just yet. You'll also have something to look back on later to see how far you've come in your healing work.

SAGITTARIUS

Outdoor activity can help you feel refreshed and promote healing, Sagittarius. As a fire sign, you may need to turn to more strenuous activities to help you release pent-up anger, energy, and emotions. When you feel physically tired, you may also feel calmer, happier, and find it easier to think things through. Getting outdoors can be especially healing for your sign.

AQUARIUS

One simple way for your sign to promote healing is to get offline. Scheduling time away from your phone, computer, and other devices can help you focus on your own healing at your own pace.

It can benefit your mental health and boost your confidence. You might decide to avoid screens entirely for a certain amount of time each day, giving you time to focus on healing activities, or just limit your social media use for the sake of your own healing.

CAPRICORN

Breathwork is a simple way for your sign to promote healing. You can sometimes be an overthinker, but you also have a lot of ambition and discipline on your side. That's why breathwork can be so effective for your sign—it's something that you can work at and practice, and you'll continue to see better and better results over time. You'll calm your nervous system and help promote both body and mind healing for yourself.

PISCES

An easy way for you to promote healing, Pisces, is by creating a healing routine for yourself. You'll often turn to creative outlets to process and heal effectively, which is up to you individually to pursue—whether you enjoy music, art, or something else entirely. But in the midst of this, you should ground yourself with a healing routine—with Neptune as your ruling planet, you may find that nighttime is best for this. Give yourself time for a calming physical activity (like yoga or stretching), self-care (from bubble baths to brushing your teeth), and something for your mind (like journaling or reading). This will help you regain more energy, sleep better, and help your mind recover and care for itself during the healing process

THESE 3 ZODIAC SIGNS JUST WANT A QUIET LIFE

CANCER

It's probably no surprise to you that you're ready for a quiet life, Cancer. As a sensitive empath, you're often overwhelmed with the world around you. Generally, your sign tends to dislike the idea of being extremely well-known or famous. Your sign is also more likely to be content with your personal successes and unswayed by what others tell you that you should be. As a person who's likely fairly introverted or at least enjoys some peace and quiet every now and then, you think you'd really enjoy the quiet life. You'd like to live in a relaxed area, have space from the people around you, and enjoy a slow, easy life with the ones you care about.

PISCES

As someone who is highly focused on creativity and dreams, you need a place you can truly relax in. Though you're often fueled by others' creativity, you also tend to be relatively sensitive and very in tune with your emotions. Being around other people constantly can be stressful, and you might often feel like you just want to get away for a while. If this is true for you, you'd probably enjoy a quiet life. You might like living in a rural area or on a property that's slightly isolated from other people. You'd enjoy having all of your creative pursuits around you and living comfortably with those you love. Not only would this bring you peace and fulfillment, it would also prevent your creative spirit from burning out.

TAURUS

You're very invested in looking for a quiet life for yourself. You seek out creature comforts like a cozy bed, homemade comfort food, and time spent with family. You love being in nature, so a space with a garden, backyard, or that has nature surrounding it is a dream come true for you. Unlike other signs that seek a quiet life, your sign may also be highly content in a cozy city apartment, even if it's a little crowded around you. That's because you enjoy transforming any space into your own, and your sign tends to find the meaning of a quiet life more about how you choose to incorporate comfort into your space.

THESE TAROT CARDS ARE TELLING YOU TO LET GO

DEATH

The Death card appears when you are about to undergo a significant life change. This change can sometimes be difficult, but you need to accept it and let go in order to experience its full benefit. The Death card appears to remind you that—even during the hardest changes—you will eventually overcome the change, feel settled, and experience significant growth and positive outcomes.

Death often represents the closing of a major life chapter. Prepare to have something huge in your life shift. It might be something that's very difficult for you to accept or it might be something that you've been ready to let go of for a while. Regardless, understand that Death is telling you that the best thing you can do for yourself is to let go, move forward, and see what new positive changes life has to offer you.

THE HANGED MAN

The Hanged Man appears when you are feeling stuck in your ways. Perhaps you are frustrated with your current life or feel unable to make a change. But the card is here to remind you that it is time to let go and change your life. You've been hanging onto the things that are no longer serving you, and now you feel bound to them. The Hanged Man shows you the reality of the situation; it is time to move on to new things.

Whether you are stuck in a dead relationship or having trouble advancing your career, the Hanged Man is a reminder that a fresh start can be a positive thing. It aims to bring you the idea that not all change is bad, and that letting go can be a good advancement for your personal growth and life satisfaction.

THE EIGHT OF CUPS

The Eight of Cups is more about letting go of the past than anything. By allowing yourself to forgive your past and close your old wounds, you make more room for the present. If you receive the Eight of Cups, it's often a sign that you need to let go of past experiences and memories that are no longer serving you. Maybe you've been spending too much time in the past or are struggling to fully let go of something you no longer have.

This card can also come around the time of an abandonment, though this is often seen as a positive thing when it comes to the Eight of Cups. Perhaps you're letting go of an old job that wasn't satisfying or a hobby you no longer cared about. Allowing yourself to let go of these things, move forward, and focus on the present is the lesson the Eight of Cups aims to teach you.

THESE TAROT CARDS MEAN EMOTIONAL GROWTH IS COMING TO YOU

THE KNIGHT OF CUPS

The Knight of Cups is all about positive change. Because it is a card in the Cups suit, it deals heavily with emotions. The Knight of Cups intuitively—and adventurously—leads the way towards emotional change and growth. It indicates that something positive is on the horizon. The Knight of Cups brings these new ideas and emotions to you; it gives you the opportunity to explore for yourself and grow quickly.

You're likely to find new opportunities for yourself when you pull this card, and the Knight of Cups wants you to welcome these things with open arms. This means that the Knight of Cups is also about opportunities that could lead you towards new emotional growth. Maybe you're about to take the next step in your relationship or have just started a new job; the Knight of Cups indicates that there are many ways you can accept emotional growth from these positive opportunities, no matter what they are.

THE EMPRESS

The Empress is an emotional teacher. She is a nurturer and a lover, and she wants you to be, too. She teaches you how to support others—and how to receive that support graciously in return—and she wants you to care deeply for your loved ones. This can lead you to significant emotional growth.

The Empress can also bring about many new opportunities for you. If you're seeking emotional growth, the Empress may signify that you're about to experience something that will lead to new emotional heights for you. Especially if you are looking to deepen the bonds you have with others (and learn how to protect them), the Empress is a fantastic card to receive. She shows you how to allow your new emotional growth to extend to those you care about.

THE PAGE OF CUPS

The Page of Cups signifies new beginnings. It is another Cups card, which means it is all about emotions. It is also a highly positive card; it shows you that you are on the path to deep growth and new opportunities. If you've been seeking emotional healing and growth, the Page of Cups is a good card to receive; it means that you will soon reap the benefits of your hard work and will see new emotional insights in the near future.

The Page of Cups can also be highly related to the inner mind and the workings of the subconscious. This can be a beneficial tie-in to emotional growth as well; you might find that the Page of Cups comes to you after extensive shadow work, healing work, or reflection. These things can all pave the way to new emotional growth—and the Page of Cups indicates that the work you're doing is highly effective.

MANIPULATION & TOXIC RELATIONSHIPS

The truth about your toxic relationship.

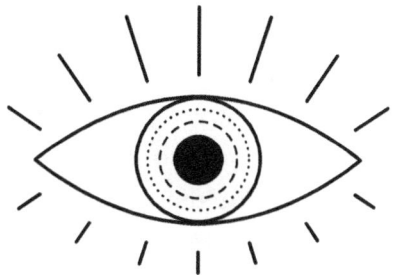

THESE 3 ZODIAC SIGNS ARE MOST LIKELY TO BE MANIPULATED

CANCER

Cancer, you're a sensitive sign who loves to nurture those you care about. When it comes to manipulation, you're likely to fall victim to those who want to take advantage of your sign's kindness and loyalty. Your sign also tends to prioritize others over yourself, which may mean that you find it difficult to refuse manipulative requests or accidentally fall victim to unhealthy relationship dynamics.

Your sign's strength when it comes to resisting manipulation is that Cancers tend to be empaths, so your intuition can guide you in determining who is really trustworthy. The only downside is that you can also often be an anxious side, which may lead you to doubt your own instincts. Observe your relationships with those you care about from outside perspectives as well as your own; you would never treat your loved ones in the way a manipulator would treat you, so do your best to recognize signs that someone might be taking advantage of your sign's caring attitude.

LIBRA

Libra, you're a graceful individual who values doing what's right above all else. You're also a mediator at heart who wants to avoid personal conflicts at all costs. This can make it easier for you to fall victim to manipulation, especially in public. You might feel nervous or awkward about speaking up against someone using manipulation tactics, especially in a group setting—your sign's natural inclination is to keep the peace, even if you're left wondering whether or not you were right to do so later on. You might also feel more inclined to put up with these kinds of behaviors just so that you don't have to confront someone taking advantage of you.

It might be useful to keep in mind, Libra, that you don't necessarily have to have a big confrontation in order to cut toxic relationships out of your life. Doing a slow fade or 'grey-rocking' a manipulator (avoiding giving any kind of personal insight or information) might help you to refuse their tactics without confronting them face-to-face. Keep in mind, though, if you do conflict with a manipulator at some point, that it's not a bad idea for you to practice setting your boundaries and standing your ground should it come to that.

TAURUS

Taurus, your sign is likely to fall victim to manipulation when it comes from someone you're comfortable around. You prioritize stability and security no matter what. This doesn't just involve your environment or your daily routine; it also occurs with the people you're used to having around. Even though you might subconsciously recognize that it's time to cut certain relationships out of your life, you can find it extremely difficult to do so when you rely on a manipulator for comfort and security. To you, that's stepping outside of your comfort zone to the extreme; you're removing someone you care about in a way that makes you feel uncomfortable and insecure. This leaves more room for manipulators to take advantage of you, because they know you won't want to leave.

Your loyalty is a major positive of your sign's personality, Taurus, but you can always try to divide your attention between multiple personal relationships at once to keep yourself in balance if you need to cut a toxic relationship out of your life. Try to ensure you have multiple friends and family members to reach out to if you need support or advice; this can make it easier for you to adjust to cutting a manipulator out of your regular routine. You may also benefit from slowly seeing them less and less, giving yourself time to adjust to life without them (and time to experience the positives of no longer having them around). The best thing you can do for yourself is to focus on change and growth when it comes to your relationships, even if you want to prioritize comfort in the moment.

HERE ARE 3 ZODIAC SIGNS THAT WILL ALWAYS PLAY VICTIM

SCORPIO

It's not uncommon for Scorpio to play the victim when something goes wrong on their end. Whether they genuinely feel that they're the wronged party or they just know how to garner sympathy, Scorpio prefers to be in control of every situation. If they have to twist a few perspectives to gain favor, they don't usually see much wrong with that. That's not to say that Scorpio is naturally untrustworthy; once you've become close to Scorpio, their true self becomes more and more apparent. But they are sometimes prone to manipulation in order to control social situations, and their natural magnetism makes it all the easier for them to do so. The best thing to do is to offer genuine conversation and authenticity to Scorpio; they often appreciate open dialogues and the chance to discuss things one-on-one.

LEO

Leo is an attention-loving sign, and this also means that they may genuinely feel that they've been wronged when someone goes against them, especially in a group setting. Their perspective can often be an emotional one, stemming from how they perceived the situation and how they reacted emotionally. This makes them play the victim more often than not, even if they're doing so unintentionally. They may genuinely see certain actions as a slight against them, causing them to take the role of the victim as a way of getting others to see their side of things and understand their emotional perspective. The best thing to do is talk to Leo one-on-one after giving them some time to themselves; they're a generous and reasonable sign after they've had some time to reflect.

TAURUS

Taurus is a stubborn bull more often than not. When they play the victim, they're hardly even putting on an act—they genuinely feel an emotionally angry and upset reaction more often than not. When wronged or when they perceive that they've been wronged, they often feel as though the entire world is against them. This can cause them to lash out instead of apologizing, making themselves out to be the hurt party. In the moment, from Taurus's perspective, this is the truth—they don't like being rattled, and a change in their emotional relationships can feel like a major change in their routine, which is discomforting to Taurus. The best thing to do is to wait out Taurus's temper and give them time to come around on their own.

THESE TAROT CARDS INDICATE YOU'RE IN A TOXIC RELATIONSHIP

If you've been getting a bad feeling when it comes to your relationship, you might have turned to tarot cards to answer any questions you have. When performing a love reading, there are plenty of cards that can arise and make you feel a little nervous—especially if you think you're in a healthy relationship. The truth is, there are lots of different meanings to every card—and even the cards listed below have positive meanings, too. If you're in a happy, healthy relationship, pulling them is not a be-all-end-all.

However, if you do feel like you might be in a toxic relationship or are looking for advice when it comes to breaking things off, the cards might have more to say about you and your partner. This is the perfect time to look out for cards that indicate that your situation might be more dire than it seems. If your intuition is telling you that you are in a toxic relationship, these are the cards you need to watch out for.

SEVEN OF SWORDS

The Seven of Swords appears to warn you about a person who is taking advantage of you. If you receive the Seven of Swords upright in a love reading, it may indicate that the person you are in love with is not who you think they are. This card may be trying to indicate that you are being manipulated or lied to.

The Seven of Swords card might also indicate that you yourself might be feeling insecure about your relationship or feel that your relationship is not fulfilling you in some way. This card may appear to warn you of your own romantic issues that are turning your relationship toxic, whether you're withdrawing from your partner due to your own insecurities or are with someone who you subconsciously know isn't right for you. The Seven of Swords may be trying to open you up to a new way of examining your relationship.

THE DEVIL

The Devil often appears relating to a controlling, manipulative relationship. It may indicate that you yourself base your relationship off of being able to manipulate your partner, or it may be trying to warn you that your partner enjoys having complete control over you.

Often, the Devil appears to those who are already in unhealthy relationships—especially if they feel 'stuck' with a toxic partner. The Devil is there to remind the querent that they, too, have control over themselves; to look at their situation with new eyes and rely on themselves to change it.

EIGHT OF SWORDS

The Eight of Swords is most likely to appear to you if you feel as though you are stuck in their current relationship. You may feel like you are unable to leave (or 'escape') your partner, as though your relationship is causing you more pain than it is worth. This is often an indicator that a querent is in a toxic relationship.

The good news is that the Eight of Swords also appears to remind you that you have the power to change your current situation—and that you should continue to move forward, taking matters into your own hands as best you can.

IF YOU'VE PULLED THESE TAROT CARDS, YOU'RE IN A TOXIC FRIENDSHIP

If you have a feeling you're in a toxic friendship, well, you probably already know subconsciously that you are. Maybe you feel like your friend is using you, manipulating you, or just doesn't seem to care about you as much as you care about them.

These feelings might lead you to pursue a tarot reading focused on your friend. Performing a reading can help guide your feelings about the situation; the cards may advise you on how to heal yourself, how to withdraw from the relationship, or how to navigate the obstacles ahead of you. They may also reassure you that everything will turn out well in the end.

If you want to look out for signs of a toxic relationship within your tarot cards, there are a few specific cards to keep in mind. Just know that every tarot card has multiple meanings; receiving these cards in a friendship you trust and know is healthy doesn't necessarily mean it's toxic. But if you have a bad feeling about a friendship you're in and are looking for reassurance, guidance, or confirmation, these are the cards you should keep an eye out for.

SEVEN OF SWORDS

If you receive this card in a friendship reading, it's likely to mean that your friend is using you for something. The friendship may not have started out this way, but now they are lying to you or manipulating you for their own gain. They could be using you to get what they want personally, professionally, or socially. They may also be manipulating you to hide an important truth from you.

The Seven of Swords advises you to use caution and stay alert when it comes to this friendship. Keep your boundaries in mind and do not allow yourself to fall victim to lies and manipulation. Set firm expectations from yourself and your friend to protect yourself, and withdraw from any relationships that feel fake or toxic.

THE DEVIL

This card has many, many meanings. But if you receive it in a friendship reading, it could be a bad sign. It often indicates manipulation and that another person is in control of you. If you feel trapped in a bad friendship or like you are not in control of yourself whenever you are around your friend, the Devil may be warning you that it is time to break away from the friendship and take care of yourself instead.

Even if you're not being manipulated, the Devil also represents codependency. Maybe you feel like you're unhealthily entangled with a friend of yours; like they're holding you back or you rely on one another to both of your detriments. The Devil can be a sign that this unhealthy pattern is leading to negative outcomes on both sides of the friendship. This card could appear to remind you that you must untangle yourself from these unhealthy relationships and grow as your own person outside of them.

TEN OF SWORDS

The Ten of Swords often indicates a betrayal. This could mean that a friend you trusted or cared about will do something hurtful that will end the friendship. This card can also be an indicator that things will not end easily; that you may need to make the decision to end the friendship (or that you will have it ended for you) and that it will hurt you.

Just remember that the Ten of Swords is also a reminder that, once the betrayal and pain of your lost friendship is over, you will begin a new chapter of your life and grow again. The betrayal can only happen once; it will allow you to grow yourself and break free of your toxic friendship in the end. Though the Ten of Swords can be a scary card to receive, it also invites you to start a new chapter for yourself once your toxic friendship has ended.

THIS IS WHAT THE DEVIL TAROT CARD REALLY MEANS

One of the Devil card's key meanings is obsession (which is sometimes described as addiction in relation to this tarot card). Typically, the goal of the Devil card is to point out a negative obsession that is consuming parts of your life. This may be a literal addiction or something that you don't directly perceive as an addiction—a toxic friend, an unhealthy romantic relationship, habits or vices that aren't serving you.

Surprisingly, though the Devil often represents feeling trapped, stuck, or powerless, the Devil can also be a reminder that you are the only person who can change your current situation. The Devil might appear to those who are struggling with bad habits, loneliness, fear, and helplessness. The Devil typically encourages the querent to allow themselves to take their situation back into their own hands, assessing their needs and forming an action plan for themselves.

The Devil can also often signify self-serving or self-indulgent behaviors. If there's behavior that you haven't noticed about yourself or patterns in your life you're already trying to change, the Devil may be pointing those out to you.

At the same time, many querents choose to embrace the self-indulgent aspects that the Devil brings. If you've been working hard on balancing out your life and making sure to choose yourself—by setting boundaries, giving time for self-care, and prioritizing your wellbeing—then it's possible that the Devil could simply be present as recognition for your hard work.

Because the Devil also represents pleasure, luxury, and materialism, you'll have to decide for yourself if the card is trying to indicate that you should take a step back or take a gentle step forward into these kinds of behaviors. The Devil does often represent over-indulgence, so be mindful when looking into your behaviors to see where the Devil might be trying to warn you of something. Some querents, however, like to use the Devil to indulge in pleasure and even materialism for a little while before returning to their normal cautious state once more.

The Devil card can also be seen as a sign of your shadow self rising. This interpretation isn't uncommon. If you've been sensing behaviors or desires that you've been repressing, the Devil may be warning you that it's time to resolve these internal conflicts—or at least acknowledge them within yourself.

When it comes to receiving an upright Devil card, you don't necessarily need to take it as a negative sign. Pair the Devil with the other cards and try to focus on what the Devil might be warning you about. Find the focus—finance? career? emotions? romance? family?—and then hone in on the things you feel most relate to the Devil card. From there, it's up to you on how to act and change your situation for the better.

If you receive a reversed Devil card, this means that you've successfully freed yourself from what is no longer serving you. You've been hard at work severing your attachments to your addictions, your vices, and/or your bad habits; you've recognized your patterns and have put in the work. You are in a state of power, abundance, and success.

IF YOUR ZODIAC SIGN IS ON THIS LIST, YOU MIGHT BE A TOXIC PARTNER

SCORPIO

You may or may not be surprised to see yourself here, Scorpio. Though you're a great painter in terms of being introspective and connecting with someone else deeply, you can also be manipulative or even controlling at times. Even when you don't know it, you might find yourself acting in ways that just aren't healthy—whether it's disguised jealousy or just plain anxiety you're trying to manage.

You can check yourself before you hurt your relationship by addressing the root of these behaviors, though. You might want to work through these learned actions with a professional or start by working through things on your own time. Open communication with your partner about what sets you on edge and what you want to change, and you might find yourself switching out your behaviors relatively quickly.

TAURUS

You might be a toxic partner when it comes to your stubbornness and deep emotional reactions, Taurus. Though typically grounded and practical, you're the sign of the bull for a reason—you lash out when you feel hurt and make it other people's problems. When you feel safe enough in your relationship to do this to your partner, you only end up hurting them in the process. It's a cruel irony, isn't it?

Your best bet might be to self-isolate when you're upset. Though this can seem counterintuitive, letting your partner know that you need to cool off and walk away could save your relationship. Work through things on your own time and only address them with your partner when you feel completely ready.

LIBRA

Though you're a sign that can attract toxic partners, you may also find yourself with toxic relationship traits yourself. Because you like to avoid conflict and dissolve tension whenever possible, you may accidentally (or maybe purposefully) veer into controlling territory in an effort to keep all conflicts to a minimum. As someone who is also a highly charming, graceful, and social sign, you may come off as manipulative, especially when it comes to social situations with or without your partner present.

To rectify these behaviors, you'll need to focus on your need to resolve conflict. Addressing anxieties and issues openly with your partner can help; creating an environment where conflicts aren't arguments to fear but instead obstacles to conquer together can also help you reframe your mindset when it comes to mediation.

Additionally, as a sign who is judicial in nature, make sure the solutions you're coming up with are actually fair to both you and your partner. A quick resolution doesn't always make a happy relationship.

THESE THREE ZODIAC SIGNS ARE MOST LIKELY TO ATTRACT TOXIC PARTNERS. HERE'S HOW TO AVOID THEM

CANCER

As a sensitive sign who struggles to set boundaries, you might not be surprised to hear that you can sometimes attract the wrong kinds of partners. Whether you get too invested early on in the relationship or are just too caring to people who don't care about you, you might find yourself feeling emotionally connected to someone who is trying to create a toxic relationship. This can make it hard for you to feel comfortable dating in the future.

To avoid this, try setting direct boundaries early on and asking for help from friends and family to hold you accountable. You can practice setting boundaries with (and on) your friends to become more comfortable speaking your mind. Additionally, you may want to set some boundaries for yourself on the support you will and won't provide to other people as you get to know them. This can help ward off anyone who wants to use you for the care you so lovingly provide to the people you like.

LIBRA

Though you don't usually have a hard time doing what's right for yourself, you do sometimes struggle with setting boundaries and discussing conflicts head-on. You're a natural mediator, which is a huge talent your sign is graced with. However, people who see that can sometimes take it to mean that you'd be easy to manipulate.

When you find yourself with a partner or date who never lets you get your way, don't feel shy about withdrawing from a tense situation to plan your next move. Space and time can help you think through a situation (and search for advice when you need it) and might help you feel calmer when addressing an issue. You should also focus on ways to make yourself feel more comfortable when involved with a conflict (even if you didn't create it)—but if you find yourself agreeing to things just to end a tense situation, practice walking away or cutting arguments short in other ways.

PISCES

As a sign who's a romantic at heart and is always searching for your soulmate, you might be prone to anyone who seems to form a deep connection with you early on, gives you romantic gifts, and wants to spend all their free time with you. Though these can seem like good signs at the start of a relationship, they're also tactics anyone who wants to get you emotionally attached to them might use. This sets you up to be ghosted or entwined in a toxic relationship later on.

Since you're already interested in finding true love at first sight, you can keep the romance story going without subjecting yourself to toxic relationships by taking things nice and slow. Pull back from anyone who seems to be cruising way too fast (or investing themselves too much at the start of a relationship) and take off those rose-tinted glasses when you think about potential partners. Slowing things down will help to weed out anyone who isn't genuinely interested in you.

THESE TAROT CARDS ARE TELLING YOU'RE BEING MANIPULATED

THE MAGICIAN, REVERSED

Receiving the Magician reversed is typically a warning about manipulation. Specifically, the card represents someone who will try to use lies, deceit, and manipulation to get something from you.

When you receive the Magician reversed, it is trying to warn you that someone in your life is not who you think they are. It may be advising you to take a look at the person who you think is manipulating you and reassess your relationship with them; for example, you may want to bow out of a planned trip or project with this person, whether they be a friend or a coworker. This card is guiding you to understand that someone you initially trusted does not have your back anymore; the Magician wants to warn you to protect yourself and put yourself first.

SEVEN OF SWORDS

The Seven of Swords is a hallmark card that indicates everything is not as it seems. If you're worried about a friend manipulating you, the Seven of Swords is a sure sign that you should be on the lookout for indications that you are being manipulated. Keep in mind that this could include anyone from someone in your personal life to someone in your professional field.

The Seven of Swords represents deception, scheming, and immorality. Someone may be using you to get what they want. They may plan on manipulating you to help them achieve their goals, or they may be using dishonesty and falsehoods to manipulate a situation or social circle you are a part of. The Seven of Swords is a warning to closely examine those around you and be wary of anyone who seems to be using you for their own gain.

THE HANGED MAN

The Hanged Man has many meanings, but if you feel that you are being manipulated by someone close to you, it can indicate that you are coming to the realization that it is time to break free. The Hanged Man may feel stuck now, but the card itself is about removing yourself from the patterns of behavior that haunt you.

If you feel that you are being manipulated by someone, the Hanged Man is truly a positive sign to receive. It is a reassurance that you must put yourself first and take your life into your own hands; that you may feel trapped and hurt by the relationship now, but that you can remove yourself from the situation and find healing. Whether you are yearning to break free of a stifling romantic relationship or reassess a social circle that has been manipulating you, the Hanged Man is a reminder that you can change your life for the better.

DREAMS, SUBCONSCIOUS, & THE FUTURE

Everything your hidden subconscious is really trying to tell you.

3 PSYCHIC ZODIACS WITH DREAMS THAT FEEL ALMOST PROPHETIC

PISCES

Pisces, you're ruled by Neptune—the planet of dreams and intuition. You're the sign that's most likely to have dreams that not only feel incredibly real but also mean something significant to you. Your deep empathy and natural sense of intuition allow you to connect with the subconscious realm more easily than other signs. Your dreams are vivid, full of symbols, and sometimes might even give you a glimpse into the future or provide solutions to problems you've been grappling with. Your subconscious is working through past events you might not consciously remember or even be aware of; this can cause it to predict future problems in your relationships or personal life. Dreams are a branch between the conscious and unconscious mind, and yours often has something very real to tell you. To make the most out of these prophetic dreams, consider keeping a dream journal. Writing down your dreams as soon as you wake up can help you decode the messages your subconscious is trying to send you.

SCORPIO

Scorpio, with your intense and mysterious energy, your dreams are a direct reflection of your inner world. Ruled by Pluto, the planet of transformation and the subconscious, you have a natural ability to visit the deepest corners of your psyche through your dreams. Your dreams are often intense and can sometimes serve as a tool for self-transformation and healing. They might reveal your deepest fears, desires, and secrets, offering you a chance to confront and work through them. Be on the lookout for recurring nightmares, themes, or motifs, as these could give you insight into what has your subconscious troubled. Trusting your intuition and paying close attention to your dreams can help your waking life, too.

CANCER

Cancer, as a water sign ruled by the Moon—the celestial body that governs emotions and intuition—your dreams are deeply connected to your emotional state. Your dreams are often a reflection of your feelings, and they can sometimes be prophetic, particularly when it comes to matters of the heart. You might find that you dream about loved ones, both past and present; these dreams can offer comfort, closure, or even warnings about potential issues in your relationships. If your dreams are being visited by the same person frequently, this may be your subconscious attempting to seek closure or reassurance from this person that it's not receiving in real life. When you're no longer able to interact with that person outside of your dreams, you'll need to reflect on what parts of the relationship your subconscious is still trying to resolve, and work through them on your own. Your dreams will come as prophecies when involving those you're close to, but they'll also give you the means to support yourself when you're no longer close with those people anymore.

GROWTH IS COMING IF YOU'VE PULLED THESE TAROT CARDS

There are many cards within the tarot deck that can symbolize growth and new chapters of your life. There's no limit on the types of growth that the tarot card might indicate for you; whether you're beginning a new passion, shedding something that no longer serves you, or just reaching a natural close to a chapter in your life, the cards you pull might have something to tell you about when (and why) you'll be experiencing growth next.

THE FOOL

The Fool is an interesting tarot card—though its name seems like a negative, the Fool is actually a happy card. The Fool is known to represent new beginnings; it's a big sign that something in your life is about to turn over a new leaf. The Fool might represent the beginning of a new project, the start of an adventure, or an event that will push you out of your comfort zone. Whatever your growth period may be, the Fool is an encouraging card; he wants you to experience the joys of the world, even if taking that first step seems challenging.

THE EMPRESS

The Empress is a card with many meanings. She often signifies fertility and maternal care. She's sometimes used to represent divine or feminine energy. But she can also indicate that a new period of growth is coming into your life. The Empress is known to rule over the creative aspects of your life, so she may indicate that new inspiration, projects, or passions are heading your way. She often signifies new potential avenues or opportunities in all aspects of your life, and, when upright, is a positive card to see when it comes to growth.

THE WHEEL OF FORTUNE

The Wheel of Fortune is all about growth and renewal. When upright, it signifies that a major positive shift will be entering your life soon. The Wheel of Fortune knows that life is about cycles; we cannot stay the same throughout our lives, but instead must fluctuate through the good and bad times. When the Wheel Of Fortune is upright, it means you may soon see a positive shift in your own fortune; things you have been struggling with may suddenly change for the better, and you may see quick results from your own growth over these periods.

THE TOWER

The Tower is often hailed as a terrifying card to receive. It's sometimes known to be a destructive one. The Tower is not just a mere change but rather a complete upheaval; it has the power to completely change the structure of your life's fundamentals. But it also means awakening and realizations, even if these come to you abruptly and chaotically. You may suddenly realize things about your own life that need to change; you may be thrust out of things that no longer serve you or violently shoved out of your comfort zone. But The Tower doesn't mean that something horrible will happen; it means that, by upheaving certain parts of your life, you make way for new change and growth to enter.

THESE 4 ZODIAC SIGNS NEED TO TRUST THEIR INTUITION RIGHT NOW

CAPRICORN

You may be a sign that follows logic over emotions most of the time, but right now, you need to trust your gut. There might be a major decision you're trying to make in your personal life or related to your career—if you find that, no matter how much time you spend weighing your options, your heart is still trying to defy the most logical solution, then you just might have your answer already.

You're likely to experience a decision that will throw you sometime soon, Capricorn. It might not be related to a major life change, but it will be something that you'll struggle with on a personal level. Don't be afraid to consult your intuition and trust your gut. It's time to rely on your subconscious and trust yourself to choose what's right for you.

PISCES

Your sign is likely to feel a subconscious pull towards something in your life this month, Pisces. It could be another person, a new career path, a random opportunity, or even a spark of inspiration related to your hobby. You're always a dreamer, so you might feel inclined to ignore your intuition and keep on thinking. But now is the time to act, Pisces.

Thanks to your ties to Neptune and your ability to connect with your subconscious mind, you may also want to sleep on any major life decisions you're trying to make within the next month. Follow your heart, but give yourself time to commune with your subconscious self and understand what your gut is trying to tell you.

AQUARIUS

You may soon be thrust into a situation where you have to make a snap decision, no matter how small. Trusting your intuition will lead you towards minor positive changes in your life, whether you improve your relationship with someone or gain some extra respect in your career.

Your sign often chooses logic over everything, but it's good to prove that you can think with your heart every once in a while. If your gut is telling you something, don't ignore it in favor of your mind this time. Be honest with yourself about what you want and what you think is best. Remember, your intuition can be based on things you haven't consciously noticed or experiences you can't even remember. It's not always illogical to follow what your gut tells you.

LEO

Leo, this month you might try to make a decision only to be at odds with yourself. You might be losing sleep over a major decision or just confused on why you're disagreeing with yourself over something seemingly small. You're used to being confident, powerful, and sure of yourself—so it can be disorienting to have to rely on your intuition when you're not exactly sure what to do.

When you're faced with a situation where your brain is telling you one thing and your soul is telling you another, follow your intuition. Listen to what your subconscious is saying and trust your instincts. They will lead you to new opportunities and more substantial successes.

THESE TAROT CARDS MEAN YOUR SHADOW SELF IS EMERGING

THE HIGH PRIESTESS

The High Priestess is all about divine femininity, intuition, and your subconscious. She tells you to trust yourself; the High Priestess does not give you the answer but rather tells you that you already know it, whether consciously or subconsciously. The High Priestess is a sacred card for many, but she can also represent the fact that your shadow self is emerging or needs to be worked on.

Your shadow self may know things about you that you haven't consciously recognized or addressed yet. For example, if you ask your tarot deck about your inner fears, about a reaction to something you had, or about a current challenge you face and you receive the High Priestess in response, she may be telling you that the answer to your problems stems from within yourself. This is what shadow work is all about; addressing your subconscious to promote healing and inner balance.

THE DEVIL

The Devil can be a mixed card, often signifying that you will face challenges ahead. It might warn you of being overly jealous, angry, or indulgent. You may give in to your vices. Some believe that the Devil card can also be about being intentionally indulgent and allowing yourself to live more freely.

The Devil card can also be about shadow work. It's about finding balance within yourself, and the best way to do this is by confronting your subconscious mind, bringing to light the things within your soul that were previously hidden. Approaching your shadow self can bring you freedom. The Devil is a card that allows you to indulge, but not overindulge—to recognize yourself in your entirety and find a way to balance every part of you, both good and bad. The Devil card may also appear as a warning that your shadow self is overtaking you; a reminder to focus on healing and processing negative emotions before they destroy your wellbeing.

THE MOON

The Moon is a tarot card that is highly mysterious. Above all else, it is a card that represents illusions and fear. This is a card that is heavily related to your shadow self, because it implies that your fears are changing the way you see reality, whether consciously or unconsciously. The Moon advises you to dive deep within yourself and uncover the way that your internal desires, your fears, and your subconscious are affecting your reality. There are so many things about yourself that you may not consciously know or have connected to your present world; the Moon wants you to bring these things into the light and examine them for what they are.

The Moon can often be about deception or secrets, but it does not always have to be. The Moon can be a card about those around you if the situation applies; but it is often more about your inner self than your external one. Look within and see what your shadow self is hiding from you; allow the Moon to help you reveal it and bring both worlds into harmony.

WHAT YOU'RE BEST AT MANIFESTING, ACCORDING TO YOUR ZODIAC SIGN

ARIES: HEALTH

Let's face it, Aries—there's actually a lot you're great at manifesting. Finances, career achievements, and awards all come easy to you. But the most unique thing about your zodiac sign is that you have an uncanny way of manifesting health. Your sign tends to prioritize using up all your energy and enjoying a multitude of physical activities, and your care for your mental and physical wellbeing might be the reason why your sign manifests health so well. When you have your energy, your mental health, and your physical being in mind at the start of each day, it's no wonder your sign is the best at manifesting health.

TAURUS: WEALTH

Under Venus's rule, you can't help but attract material wealth. Whether you're busy envisioning your dream home (and then eventually achieving it) or have set your sights on saving a certain amount of money, you're going to achieve it one way or another. As a grounded sign, you're likely to focus deeply on your goals and know your true desires well. This, along with your ruling planet, makes you the best zodiac sign to attract money.

GEMINI: FRIENDSHIPS

As a social sign, you're undoubtedly the best at manifesting new friendships. That's because you're naturally extroverted and love connecting with others—you draw other people to you, not the other way around. You come across as friendly, interesting, and fun to talk to—and you're able to manifest new relationships because of your extensive social circle and line of hobbies that you can rely on.

CANCER: LOVE

You're best at manifesting platonic and familial love, Cancer. You care deeply about others and value close, long-term relationships—you'd rather have one or two best friends than a huge group of acquaintances. Because you care so much and so well for others, the universe gives that energy right back to you, making it easy for you to manifest love for yourself.

LEO: FAME

You don't need to be a superstar in order to manifest fame, Leo. Whether you achieve fame within your career, your social circle, your local community, or even as a family legend, you're bound to attract fame one way or another. Your sign can't help but love being in the spotlight, so you're sure to draw fame to you (even by accident).

VIRGO: ACCOLADES AND ACHIEVEMENTS

Thanks to your organization and goal mindset, achievements come easy to you. You're likely to find professional success thanks to projects you've worked on—or you might receive personal awards related to your hobbies or interests. You dedicate yourself so deeply to the things you care about, you end up manifesting many achievements for yourself along the way.

LIBRA: YOUR CAREER

One thing that you're great at manifesting is your professional life. As a Libra, you might have a specific dream for yourself in mind that you want to achieve—this could have been instilled in you from a young age or something you suddenly realize you want to pursue. Because of this, you're likely to manifest your dream career. It's something you think about all the time, so you naturally pull it towards you.

SCORPIO: MATERIAL POSSESSIONS

It's said that Scorpio manifestations work best when they are highly specific. This might mean that your sign does best at manifesting material possessions. If you can think about it, know exactly what it looks like, feels like, its cost, why you want it, where you'd put it, what you'd do with it—well, Scorpio, you're much more likely to get it than other signs. You need to focus completely on your manifestations, but when you want something, you will receive it.

SAGITTARIUS: ADVENTURE

It's probably not much of a surprise that you're best at manifesting new horizons for yourself. That's because you've always got freedom on the mind. The perfect trip might fall in your lap coincidentally, or you might spot a sudden opportunity to visit your dream hike. When you embrace adventure, you manifest it.

CAPRICORN: YOUR GOALS

Achieving your goals is your number one manifestation, Capricorn. It's what your sign was built to do. If you want to become professionally successful, boost your finances, or even set a basic personal goal for yourself, you manifest it so perfectly, you just have to achieve it—no doubt about it.

AQUARIUS: NEW INSPIRATION

You're always looking for something new to inspire you, whether in your professional life or when working on a creative project or hobby. This means that you somehow manifest inspiration, finding it in odd places you never thought you would. Whether you dream up a new idea or randomly realize something essential to your work, you're amazing at manifesting inspiration all the time.

PISCES: ROMANCE

You're a hopeless romantic, Pisces—you just can't help it. As a dreamer and a creative, you love love. You adore romance movies, want to plan cute dates, and never fail to express your love to your partner. This makes you perfect at attracting the kind of romance you desire. You spend so much time envisioning it, you have no problems recognizing it—and achieving it.

WHAT'S HOLDING YOU BACK FROM ACHIEVING YOUR DREAMS, BASED ON YOUR ZODIAC SIGN

ARIES: YOU'RE TOO IMPATIENT.

Aries, patience is not your strong suit. You like to rush into things head-on, take risks, and take charge. Playing the long game isn't something you enjoy—you want to see results! When it comes to goals that don't have anything to show until the very end, you often struggle to keep pushing (especially when there are other projects that will get you the change you want to see much faster). To combat this, try keeping one longer goal alongside several other shorter ones. You'll be boosted by small changes while waiting for a bigger payoff.

TAURUS: YOU'RE TOO COMFORTABLE.

As a Taurus, you probably already know that you're too familiar with your comfort zone. Your sign sometimes finds it impossible to take risks, which can sometimes make achieving your goals a slow process. When it comes to tasks that require a little bit of challenge and spontaneity, you may find it difficult to stick to the plan. But you can always try making small changes one at a time, Taurus—a little risk may be easier to stomach than a big one.

GEMINI: YOU'RE TOO BUSY.

Gemini, you have a lot on your plate. As the sign of the twin, you're multifaceted—you can't help but have a million things going on at once. But being pulled in all directions makes it difficult to focus on one thing at a time. Projects that require a lot of focus and time aren't always your strong suit, especially if they take a long time and you find yourself more interested in starting something new. Still, you can always try picking up many new smaller projects while working on something more long-term as a way of keeping yourself interested.

CANCER: YOU DON'T SET BOUNDARIES.

Cancer, you've probably heard before that you need to set some boundaries with other people. But what about with yourself? There's really no such thing as being too kind to yourself, but your sign can sometimes tend to be overly lenient when it comes to achieving your goals. Hard deadlines and serious projects aren't always your forte, Cancer. If you want to work on this, try holding yourself accountable (and asking your friends or family to help). Set goals for yourself that you want to achieve in a certain way, and track your progress to ensure you'll stick to it.

LEO: YOU'RE NOT INVESTED ENOUGH.

Leo, your sign tends to have a lot of accomplishments behind you! But when you're setting goals that are completely personal and don't have much accountability, you struggle to accomplish them. The projects you perform the best on are the ones that will be seen by everyone important to you, but the goals you sometimes struggle with are more personal ones. If possible, you might want to invite other people to join you in these goals or just let them know what you're working on. This is a great way of making it so that your personal accomplishments can still be seen by the people you want to share them with.

VIRGO: YOU SET THE BAR TOO HIGH.

Virgo, if it were up to you, nothing would ever be finished. When it comes to projects that don't have a deadline or personal goals you're working on, you'll never have them perfected, so they'll never be finished. You're great when it comes to attention to detail, which should make it easier for you than most to achieve your goals. But you need to refocus your efforts on setting an end date for yourself instead of continuing to make minuscule changes. First, you can always try setting a personal goal that's constantly changing, so that you can update milestones for yourself as you achieve them. Secondly, you should also focus on creating small goals with deadlines that will ensure you won't be able to keep aiming for complete perfection on any of them, as a way of practicing imperfection.

LIBRA: YOU'RE TOO INDECISIVE.

Libra, when it comes to your personal goals, you probably have a lot of aspirations. You're a social and very professional sign, which makes you well-liked in your personal life and your career. But you also struggle when it comes to making decisions, which can sometimes make you try to achieve everything at once (even when it's not possible) or end up with nothing because you took too long to make a decision. We've all been there, Libra, and it's hard to know that you can't always have it all at once. But no decision is worse than a decision you're uncertain about. Try to ask for advice from those you trust as much as possible, so you can at least feel confident and supported in the decision you end up making.

SCORPIO: YOU'RE NOT COMMITTED.

Scorpio, you're generally good at understanding your own subconscious, and sometimes it controls your day-to-day actions, too. You might be subconsciously avoiding a goal because you're no longer aligned with it or even because you're self-sabotaging your own successes. Either way, this is something that merits some reflection on your part. When you're committed to your goals, you show it—you're dedicated and serious about your work. But when there are goals you aren't achieving, it's usually because you're just not committed to them anymore. There's often a reason why you're suddenly acting less serious about something—even if it takes some time to discover that reason, Scorpio, it's worth reflecting on to see if you need to help yourself finish off the final project or move onto something new.

SAGITTARIUS: YOU MOVE ON TOO QUICKLY.

Sagittarius, you probably have a lot of unfinished goals in your pocket. That's because you love to bounce around from one thing to another, never sticking with one project for too long. As soon as you get an idea in your head, you start working (and you usually dream big, too). But you quickly find another source of inspiration, and then another after that. You keep chasing these new projects and new goals, discarding old ones because they either no longer interest you or no longer serve you. When your interests change so fast, it can be hard for your goals to keep up! To counteract this, you can focus on either choosing extremely short-term goals or opting for longer projects that encompass multiple of your interests.

CAPRICORN: YOU'RE BURNING OUT.

Capricorn, you're basically known as the sign who accomplishes their goals no matter what. When you're struggling to finish something that's on your plate, it's probably because your plate is also filled with a million other things that your discipline just won't let you discard. It can be especially difficult for your sign to recognize burnout, because you're used to overloading yourself (and you often enjoy having too much to do). When you're not achieving your goals in the way you used to, take a step back and see if you're working on too much at once. Organize and prioritize your goals in a way that makes sense for you (and allows you some time for a little R&R). Don't overdo it, Capricorn—you'll only end up out of the field for longer later.

AQUARIUS: YOU WON'T ASK FOR HELP.

Aquarius, you can certainly be convinced to ask for advice from other professionals in your field. You sometimes enjoy conferencing with those who know exactly what you're working on (and why). But when it comes to goals where you don't have a network to speak with (and sometimes even goals where you do), you struggle to reach out and ask for help when you need it. Your sign often wants to do things on your own—you want to have all the solutions and complete your projects alone. It's satisfying for you to be the innovator and the builder. But sometimes, you need help in order to complete your goals more efficiently. That doesn't mean you can't do it all yourself, just that you might need a little extra brainpower to boost you towards the finish line. Consider asking for advice that you can implement yourself rather than outsourcing parts of the project—it will reassure you that you still have the skills to finish your goals on your own.

PISCES: YOU NEVER START THEM.

Pisces, you've often got your head in the clouds, dreaming of all the different things you want to do. You'll probably notice that when you do start a goal of yours, you're typically able to finish it—you're certainly not lacking in inspiration. But because you're such a dreamer, you sometimes spend all your time thinking about the goals you want to accomplish instead of starting them. When you do want to accomplish them later on, you may have already lost interest. You may also fall victim to the idea that you need to wait for something to happen before you can start working on your goals. This isn't always the case, Pisces. Think of a small goal for yourself you can start right away, no matter what it is. Work your way up to the larger dreams you have for yourself—just as with the things you have accomplished, these new goals will soon come easy to you.

THESE TAROT CARDS MEAN YOUR LUCK IS ABOUT TO TURN

WHEEL OF FORTUNE

The Wheel of Fortune card is the most referenced card when it comes to change, especially pertaining to luck. It may signify a drastic shift; when upright, it signals that positive change will soon be present in your life. If you've been down on your luck, the Wheel of Fortune is the card you want to see.

The Wheel of Fortune, as its name implies, is often used to symbolize a turning of luck—not just luck in general—because it's intended to represent (quite literally) the cyclical nature of luck. It demonstrates the periods of change we go through, the ups and downs of life, and often indicates that a chapter of your life is about to turn.

THE STAR

The Star is often viewed as a lucky tarot card because it indicates a period of renewal and positivity. The Star is all about bringing hope into your life, especially if you've been lacking hope or inspiration recently. This is another reason why The Star is about changing your luck; it brings you new energy when you feel you are out of strength to carry on. The Star is a sign that things are going to change for the better and that you should hold out hope for a positive future.

NINE OF CUPS

The Nine of Cups is all about wishes. It usually means good fortune to the querent and indicates that your dreams will soon be answered. The Nine of Cups usually appears when you are about to achieve a goal or ambition of yours, fulfill something that will satisfy you, or experience good fortune and abundance in your life. This is not just a changing of your luck, but a deeper bettering of your life; something major you have been working towards will be achieved for you in a way that satisfies your entire being.

THESE ZODIAC SIGNS NEED TO PAY MORE ATTENTION TO THEIR DREAMS

TAURUS

As a practical sign, you may not be familiar with analyzing your dreams or keeping a dream journal. You, Taurus, tend to be more grounded in reality than in your subconscious. But analyzing your dreams can provide you with insights that will lend you a lot of useful knowledge in the real world—not just while you sleep. As someone who's familiar with your comfort zone, learning to understand your dreams can help you make some serious strides when it comes to growth and self-improvement. Who knows, Taurus, connecting with the dream world might bring you more insights than you think.

AQUARIUS

Aquarius, if you're not paying attention to your dreams, you really should be. As an innovator, much of your inspiration and motivation can actually happen while you sleep. Convening with your subconscious while you're asleep can lend you solutions to the problems you have while you're awake—keeping track of your dreams may net you a few signs or symbols of inspiration you can use in your projects. Focusing on your dreams when you're awake can also help you notice and retain more once you're asleep.

VIRGO

For you, Virgo, dreams are a fast-track to understanding your inner workings. From things you're anxious about that you're totally unaware of to subconscious desires you have yet to manifest, there are plenty of benefits that will come from you learning to understand your dreams. As an analytical sign, you'd have no trouble adjusting to keeping a detailed log of all your dreams (and you'd probably enjoy going through each plot and symbol to create a thorough analysis, too). If you're really dedicated (and let's be honest, you very much are), you could even create a tracker to determine how your dreams change based on real-life events, periods of stress, and your energy levels.

THESE TAROT CARDS MEAN GREAT SUCCESS IS IN YOUR FUTURE

THE EMPEROR

The Emperor represents stability. If you want to achieve a happy, powerful, and secure life, then the Emperor is the card you want to see. The Emperor is often most associated with financial wealth and career success, because the Emperor typically represents power and being a leader. This means that he is often a most positive indicator of success when it comes to career or financial questions.

Though the Emperor often appears after you have achieved a position in life in which you feel secure, he can also be a good sign for the future when he appears. It may be a sign that you will come into power or that you feel that you have the power to follow your goals. He could indicate future stability and wealth. As an Emperor, this card also represents hard work. It means that you achieve your success and stability from your own efforts—they are not handed to you, but are instead made by you.

ACE OF WANDS

When it comes to future successes, the Ace of Wands might just be the card you want to see. That's because it represents the very beginning of a new journey that will eventually lead you to success. It encourages you to pursue your dreams and embark on a new adventure; it wants to see you take action, leap into the unknown, and follow your passions with trust and joy.

If you're considering a new career path for yourself, have started a new relationship, or are reaching a new chapter of your life in some way, look out for the Ace of Wands. It's a sign of encouragement that you are doing right by yourself.

SIX OF WANDS

The Six of Wands represents success in all forms. You might receive a major accolade or be recognized for a future achievement. You feel confident and self-assured that you will achieve your goals. You work towards them with the secure knowledge that you will someday achieve your goals.

Though the Six of Wands can often appear after a goal has been completed, it can also be an immensely positive sign that you will someday see the success you crave. The Six of Wands is about overcoming obstacles and returning successfully; whether you want to be financially secure, meet your soulmate, or be celebrated for your achievements, the Six of Wands is a positive sign for all.

NINE OF CUPS

The Nine of Cups is all about having your dreams be granted. If you have a goal or a hope for your future, it will come true. The Nine of Cups is reassuring you that you are on the path to success; if you have not already seen your goals met, you will someday achieve them.

The Nine of Cups can be a fantastic card to receive when it comes to future success because it can apply to many areas of your life. It can mean achieving happiness in love, finding comfort in your career, appreciating your personal life, or simply finding joy each day in the present moment. No matter when you receive this card, it is a reminder that good things are on their way to you, and that you will someday have the life you dream of.

THESE TAROT CARDS ARE SIGNS YOU'RE SELF-ACTUALIZING

THE HIGH PRIESTESS

The High Priestess can be a spiritual, mysterious, and even sacred card to pull. Though she's often shrouded in mystery, she can be a unique sign that you're on the path to self-actualization. This is because the High Priestess is a sign that the guidance you're seeking from the tarot deck is already within you.

The High Priestess is guiding you towards completing your self-actualization by allowing you to trust your instincts and follow the path you believe in your heart is best for you. This is how you can truly reach your higher self; by allowing your own mind and body to guide you there. The High Priestess can sometimes be a frustrating card to receive when you just want advice, but the truth is, she is allowing you to experience true growth and knowledge that will lead you to self-actualize as soon as you learn to trust yourself. After all, how can you become your best self if you can't even trust yourself?

THE QUEEN OF CUPS

Think of the Queen of Cups as telling you to finish filling up your own cup (or even someone else's). She is an incredibly kind person; she might represent someone you want to be (moral, helpful, caring, in control over their emotions) or someone who does what you want to do (take care of yourself and others).

She may also appear to you when you need to refocus on your wellbeing, which will allow you to self-actualize and reach your higher self later on.

The Queen of Cups is a good sign to receive when you're trying to connect with your higher self. She is there to remind you to take care of yourself along the way and to trust yourself in the journey. She is also a reminder of who your best self can be; someone who feels fulfilled by themselves and by taking care of others, too.

THE EMPRESS

The Empress governs self-expression, creativity, new life, and even romance. She can be a fantastic card to receive if you are trying to self-actualize because of how many areas of growth she represents. If you are seeking abundance, the Empress can be a great sign. If you see self-actualization occurring after finding true love, then the Empress may guide you. If you want to start a new chapter for yourself after reaching self-actualization, the Empress may be a sign that you are close to success.

The Empress is also another sign of a person who you may want to be more like; someone who values self-expression and creativity in all things. If you envision your higher self pursuing passion projects, being motivated, caring for others deeply, and enjoying healthy and fulfilling relationships (amongst other things), then the Empress may be a good reminder for you to continue your work in becoming that person.

THE QUEEN OF WANDS

The Queen of Wands is often a tarot card that a querent can look up to. She is all about having self-confidence. She trusts herself completely. She is a highly independent person who is not afraid of facing the challenges ahead of her. The message she brings is to take control over yourself and your goals. She brings you new, refreshing energy and reminds you to keep your head up no matter what; she can also be a symbol of hope to those who seek her guidance.

If you are trying to self-actualize, then the Queen of Wands is a good sign. Not only does she give you inspiring character traits to model your higher self after, but she can also be a positive sign that great things are coming your way. She advises you to be ambitious and determined, but also to look within yourself and raise your own confidence and self-esteem. These are powerful pieces of guidance when it comes to connecting with your higher self.

THESE TAROT CARDS ARE TELLING YOU TO LET YOUR INTUITION GUIDE YOU

THE HIGH PRIESTESS

The High Priestess is the tarot card with the most symbolic meaning around intuition. She appears to those who need to trust their instincts and allow their intuition to guide them. If you approach the deck with a specific question and pull the High Priestess, she is telling you that you already know the answer—you just haven't accepted it yet.

The High Priestess guides you to accept the answer your conscious mind is refusing to hear or to allow you to trust your instincts when it comes to a problem you are trying to solve. If you approach the deck and find the High Priestess waiting for you, she is likely telling you that your intuition already knows the action you need to take. She wants you to listen to yourself and rely on yourself more.

The High Priestess can also be a highly spiritual card or even a sacred card for many. She is often connected to witchcraft, the Moon, and femininity. She may not tell you the answers or advice you seek outright, but she trusts that you have the guidance she would otherwise give you already within your mind.

THE MOON

The Moon is a card that is highly connected to the subconscious, the shadow self, and mysteries. The Moon often appears to point out something that you need to reflect on; it may represent your subconscious fears and anxieties or a problem that you have been avoiding. It may show you how to heal your shadow self or give you the tools to address your subconscious.

The Moon is also deeply connected to your intuition. It asks you to rely on your intuition in the face of obstacles and uncertainty. It may appear in times of confusion to remind you to rely on yourself and trust your gut feelings.

The Moon may also try to help you bridge the gap between your conscious and unconscious mind by trusting your intuition. Your instincts may be advising you of something that your conscious mind has not yet realized. The Moon may also help you to see and better understand your intuition and your actions; it may bring harmony to your conscious and subconscious, allowing you to work on yourself and learn to trust your instincts.

THE FOOL

The Fool is all about new beginnings and new opportunities. The Fool encourages you to take risks and embrace all the possibilities of life. It's a joyful card; the Fool is not meant to be an insult to the querent but rather a celebration of innocence, risks, and new life chapters.

The Fool guides the querent to trust their intuition and take the leap. When a querent has been on the brink of making a new decision, plagued by uncertainty, or lacking trust in their own judgment or gut feelings, the Fool may appear to guide them to a new decision. The Fool may also appear to indicate that a new life change is on the horizon and encourage you to embrace it with open arms.

When it comes to making decisions, the Fool gives you the freedom to trust your intuition despite the risks. If you've been debating over something you've been wanting to do or just don't feel confident enough to trust your gut instincts, allow the Fool to guide you into taking the plunge. That doesn't mean that you can't inform yourself of the risks to make healthy decisions—but it does mean that a satisfying life is not entirely risk-free, especially when your instincts are telling you something.

HEALTH & WELLNESS

Promoting wellness throughout mind, body, and soul.

IF YOU'RE ONE OF THESE 3 ZODIAC SIGNS, YOU NEED TO WORK ON YOUR SOCIAL MEDIA ADDICTION

GEMINI

It's easy for you to get sucked into your social media feed because you're just trying to keep up with your friends, Gemini. Maybe it starts off with you checking your DMs, making a quick post, or catching up with all the people you follow, but you're an easily distracted sign—you always end up stuck in a scrolling cycle, totally losing track of time.

Your busy schedule helps you forget about your social media addiction, but you still struggle to manage it sometimes. Maybe you notice that some days you're using your phone less than others, but that's usually when your schedule gives you less free time. On your own, you have much more trouble staying away from the phone.

To help, the best thing for you to do is replace your phone with a quick hobby as often as possible. When you're at home, reach for something that's easy to get sucked into—a puzzle, an art project, a journal. On the go, make sure you have something with you that's just as appealing as your phone, like a podcast, book, or sketchpad. If you do need some tech time, try to opt for long-form content so you can manage your time better—like video essays or movies.

SCORPIO

Your sign often finds it a little too easy to fall victim to the social media trap. You tend to enjoy the mindlessness that comes with scrolling and often find it hard to put your phone down. You might even find your phone more relaxing than other hobbies, as it allows you to quickly 'turn off' your brain and zone out for a while.

Though this is harmless in small doses, your sign often finds social media affecting you in other ways. You might feel more anxious or lose hours of your day to social media. Your sign also tends to form an anxious attachment to your own phone, making it hard for you to calm your anxiety or stress naturally—you may feel like you have to turn to social media to destress at the end of the day, and if you don't, you can't relax.

You'll need to quit your phone slowly, Scorpio. Replace social media with other relaxing activities as much as possible. Your sign might even want to opt for something that requires little effort to get started, like meditation or breathwork. This can help you calm your anxiety right away and refocus on finding a new activity that is better for you than endless time spent on social media. Use social media for set periods of time, with a reminder telling you when your session is up.

SAGITTARIUS

You might be surprised you made it on this list, Sagittarius. You usually don't think of yourself as a social media addict, but it's highly likely for your sign in particular to be addicted to social media. This usually happens because you're easily distracted—you go online to look something up or talk to someone quickly but end up falling down a rabbit hole of feeds.

Once you start scrolling, you find it difficult to stop. Your sign sometimes struggles with productivity or forcing yourself to work on something you don't want to, and your phone is an easy way to distract you from that. Unfortunately, it also tends to drain all of your energy (and your schedule)—by the time you look up from your phone, you want to get going even less than you did before.

Fortunately, your sign has a good chance of being able to quit social media. You might consider going cold turkey, as that tends to work for your sign—deleting all your social media apps and telling your friends to text or call you instead. If that's not possible for you, you should set strict limits on apps so that you can only use them briefly throughout the day. Because social media drains your energy so quickly, you should consider using your screen time (or a blocker app) to set times in the morning and evening where you're not allowed to use social media. Then, add a total time limit for the day. This will help you start your day productively and prevent you from scrolling for hours in the afternoon.

WHAT SCENT YOU SHOULD WEAR, BASED ON YOUR ZODIAC SIGN

ARIES: CITRUS

Citrus is a bold, inviting, and confident scent. It's perfect for a fire sign like you—both unique and appreciated by pretty much everyone. You'll be pleased to have a go-to scent that you really can't go wrong with—and even though citrus scents can be strong, they're rarely too overpowering.

TAURUS: ROSE

The comforting smell of fresh roses should be pleasant for you, Taurus. Not only are they a floral scent—something you as an earth sign will appreciate—they're also known to be a classic and timeless scent. For someone who loves tradition, roses are perfect. Best of all, they're a beloved scent, which also makes them easy to find, ensuring that you can pick out a single perfume, soap, or scent bag that you'll never have to switch up on.

GEMINI: LAVENDER

Everyone loves lavender; it's considered a friendly, welcoming, and appealing scent. As a social butterfly, your scent might actually be pretty important to you (really, whose isn't?)—it gives you an extra sense of appeal when you're meeting new people! Lavender is a classic scent, but it's also frequently mixed with other scents, which leaves you with many new options to try when you're feeling curious.

CANCER: VANILLA

Who doesn't enjoy a sweet vanilla perfume? For many, vanilla represents love and comfort. It can be a deeply nurturing and calming scent that brings with it a caring, familiar feel. You might even have memories attached to the scent of vanilla—other loved ones that wear similar perfume or the smell of baked goods. Vanilla will give you a scent that's literally just like your sweet, sensitive personality.

LEO: AMBER

The smell of amber is a bold and musky scent, Leo. It's warm and inviting, like yourself, and it has many layers—perfect for a unique scent with plenty of self-expression. It tends to be recognized as an attractive scent, so you can steal the show whenever you please, and it's a pleasantly comforting scent for a sign ruled by the Sun.

VIRGO: EUCALYPTUS

Eucalyptus is often used as a candle or perfume base to make something smell fresh, clean, and bright. For someone who is always organized, enjoys home DIY projects, loves keeping things clean, and looks for a scent that isn't overpowering, eucalyptus is the perfect go-to. Even better, it can help you relax and even get better sleep. To wear eucalyptus, look for a perfume that uses eucalyptus as a base scent or additional perfume note. For you, Virgo, using it in your home as a diffuser, candle, dried plant, or incense will also be ideal.

LIBRA: JASMINE

Jasmine is a sweet and inviting scent, perfect for someone social like yourself. It's a light, well-balanced scent, ideal for someone who looks for harmony in all things. The nice thing about jasmine is how well it works for different scent styles; you can wear it to work, on a casual day in, or on a fancy night out. This type of flexibility and aesthetic is well-received by you, Libra.

SCORPIO: MUSK

Musk is often known for being enchanting and alluring. For a social and highly magnetic sign, you'll want a perfume that can charm people almost as well as you do. Generally, musk is almost a secret scent—it smells good, but not overly perfume-y. You, Scorpio, will likely be able to appreciate this kind of scent. Plus, its richer notes and natural spice will appeal to you and your darker aesthetics.

SAGITTARIUS: JUNIPER

Juniper is an adventurous and appealing smell. It's fresh, crisp, and is known for smelling like the outdoors. Best of all, you'll often find juniper in a wide variety of scent mixes; vanilla for a sweet and welcoming scent, bonfire or campfire for an extremely outdoorsy vibe, and other fresh mixes to smell like mountain air. Wearing juniper will literally make you smell like you just came back from a pleasantly woodsy walk.

CAPRICORN: SANDALWOOD

Sandalwood is a popular scent for a reason. It's a clean scent base for layering and it even helps to naturally lower stress levels. Some even believe that it can help in meditation. Sandalwood is a popular scent in colognes, perfumes, candles, and more. It's the perfect go-to scent for someone as ambitious as you. It's classic, smells delicious and pleasantly calming, and might even help you focus a little extra.

AQUARIUS: HONEY

Honey is a warm and sweetly unique scent. Your sign is likely to dislike strong scents or perfumes in general, so you'll want to opt for something pleasant and delicate. Honey is a solid choice because it usually isn't too strong. Natural-smelling honey scents will have an extremely gentle sweetness to them, often carrying an almost unnoticeable fresh or flowery scent to them, too. This makes them ideal for spritzing as a regular base scent, because they give you a distinct smell that doesn't smell purely like perfume.

PISCES: LEMONGRASS

Lemongrass is a fresh and pleasantly grassy scent. It smells vibrant and citrus-y, and carries a sweet scent with tons of layers. As the name implies, it's partially lemony and partially herby, making for a cheerful and inviting scent that pleases everyone. For someone who is creative, bright, emotionally intelligent, and maybe needs a little extra focus when daydreaming, lemongrass is the perfect choice.

THESE TAROT CARDS ARE URGING YOU TO GROUND YOURSELF

THE HIEROPHANT

The Hierophant is Taurus's tarot card, ruled by Venus. Taurus is known for being patient, stable, and grounded—so it makes sense that the Hierophant is also sometimes associated with roundedness. After all, it is also a card about traditions and learning. The Hierophant is also said to be connected to the Earth element through Taurus—another way that it can be a good reminder to ground yourself.

The Hierophant may be letting you know that you need to ground yourself when it comes to your values, personal practices (spiritual or otherwise), and even your passions. Perhaps you need to ground yourself in reality by pursuing your passions through a teacher, as the Hierophant would advise—or maybe you've lost track of the daily practices that can help ground you, like meditation or journaling. The Hierophant is a reminder to take care of yourself and your emotions.

JUSTICE

As a hallmark of truth, the Justice card can be a good reminder to ground yourself. It's most commonly associated with a situation where you feel like you wish you could see the truth brought to light or have justice wrought; it might reassure you that fairness will come in the end. Justice brings balance to all things, and rights the wrongs of the world.

Because of its righteous and balanced nature, Justice is often seen as a grounding card. It could come as a reminder that you yourself need to be balanced; it may appear when your own personal scales of life are unequal. Whether your emotions are running too high or you feel hopeless, the Justice card reminds you that you need to gain control over yourself, ground yourself, and trust that all will work out in the end.

KING OF CUPS

The King of Cups is truly a grounded card. As the ruler of the suit associated with emotions, the King of Cups has complete control over his emotions and displays a grounded, balanced personality. When this card arrives, it may be commending you on your control over yourself. It may also be reminding you that showing a fair and grounded persona is important—perhaps you could take more time to ground yourself in your daily life.

Keep in mind that the King of Cups is not necessarily a completely stoic figure. After all, the Cups are about showing emotion to others, nurturing, and being compassionate. Because of this, the King of Cups is seen as a kind and caring figure. Know that grounding yourself means tapping into your emotions and being in tune with them, not suppressing them entirely.

THESE TAROT CARDS ARE ENCOURAGING YOU TO PURSUE MINDFULNESS

THE MOON

The Moon is all about intuition. It often deals in secrets and even misunderstandings, but it can also be a highly powerful card when it comes to mindfulness and mental health. The Moon urges you to confront your inner anxieties and fears. It wants to bring your hidden shadows into the light—not to cause you pain, but to allow you to address them and resolve these inner anxieties.

This is a good reminder to practice mindfulness and focus on your mental health. If you've been struggling lately, have been unfocused when it comes to your healing journey, or haven't been taking time for yourself, the Moon card may appear to you. It can remind you to take the time to find inner clarity and peace.

THE HIGH PRIESTESS

It's true that the High Priestess is a sacred card for many, associated with spirituality and the moon. Although she often represents secrets and hidden truths, she can also be about achieving inner clarity and shedding light on your inner self. She wants to reveal your unconscious truths and, much like the Moon, bring both sides of yourself into balance.

Because of this, the High Priestess is often associated with mental health, meditation, and mindfulness. Her spiritual nature doesn't exclusively apply to religion or spiritual practices; it can also be about seeking calm and clarity within your own mind. The High Priestess may appear when it's time to focus on being more mindful and sorting out the inner chaos within yourself.

THE ACE OF SWORDS

The Swords suit typically deals with matters of the mind. Because of this, the Ace of Swords is a good card to receive when it comes to mindfulness. It's a reminder to focus on clearing your head and focusing on your own thoughts. It can represent new inspiration and new ideas.

The Ace of Swords can also come when you make a major realization or conclude a reflection upon yourself. It can appear when you've connected with an empowering truth—or are about to. The card also often indicates success, which can be a positive sign if you've been working on mindfulness and mental health recently.

THESE TAROT CARDS ARE ENCOURAGING YOU TO PURSUE HEALTHY HABITS

STRENGTH

Strength is all about inner healing, power, and recovery. If you have recently experienced a challenge in your life, you are also on the path to overcoming it. It combines all different types of strength together—depending on your circumstances, it could be about mental fortitude or even about your newfound physical capabilities.

Strength reminds you that you have control over yourself and that you are strong when you need to be. It encourages you to continue on a path of growth and allow yourself to explore the new chapter life has brought you. When you have recovered from your hardships—as Strength encourages you to do—it can also be about allowing yourself to grow new habits out of the old ones. Strength wants to see you rely on your mental, physical, emotional, and even spiritual capabilities to build yourself up, again and again.

THE WORLD

The World card can signify an end to an old chapter. It is about finding success and closure. The World card will likely appear to you when you have finished something big—a goal or a chapter of your life—successfully.

Now that part of your life is over, the World encourages you to continue forward and accept new growth. It celebrates the success that you have built and wants you to keep finding new energy and meaning in your life. A great way to do this is begin again by setting new goals for yourself and finding new ways you can achieve small successes every single day. By setting new intentions and new habits for yourself, you can continue to succeed and carry the lessons of the World with you.

TEMPERANCE

The Temperance card is all about bringing your life into balance. When it comes to your health, it prioritizes ensuring that there is harmony in your actions; that you are not putting too much weight on just one area of your life, tipping the scales too far. Temperance encourages you to fill all of your cups evenly; it appears when you are dedicating too much of yourself to something that is unproductive.

If you've been struggling lately, one thing that Temperance would advise would be to look at small changes within your life that you can make to bring yourself back into balance. This change may not happen immediately; Temperance is merely warning you that it must happen at some point, before you completely burn yourself out. Focusing your attention evenly on all aspects of your wellbeing and instilling well-rounded habits in yourself is exactly what Temperance aims to achieve.

THE STAR

The Star is a beacon of hope, strength, and new energy. It might come to you when you are feeling low, to assure you that there is light at the end of the tunnel. Some say that it can even be related to personal or spiritual practices, especially those that boost your energy and lift your spirits.

The Star is also a sign that things will be changing positively for you soon. It is all about having hope for the future and looking ahead to new, good things. This is a fantastic sign for you to begin changing your life in small ways. Not only does the Star bring about more energy and productivity for you, it will also give you the inspiration and self-motivation you need to begin changing your life.

SPIRITUALITY

The practicing zodiac for spiritual souls.

CHOOSE YOUR ZODIAC SIGN AND GET A HINT ABOUT YOUR PAST LIFE

ARIES

You and your past self are most connected via your ambitions and natural talents. Aries are high achievers, so there are a few options that could present in you from your past self. The first is that your past self was proud of what they accomplished and naturally skilled at something they received lots of recognition for. This would manifest itself in you the same way it did in your past self; a continuation of their greatest efforts. The second is a past Aries manifesting something they lacked in you; if they felt a part of themselves wasn't up to par, they may have reinvented a body that was skilled in ways your past self wasn't. You can tell which is which by how connected and attached to your accomplishments you feel, and what (if anything) you fear being taken away from you.

TAURUS

You can reveal the most about your past life through your stubbornness. There might be one or two topics that really grind your gears. Your sign tends to react quickly and lash out, often overreacting to minor inconveniences (especially if you're already in a bad mood). Looking into your pet peeves and particular reactions can help you decipher more information about your past life. Depending on where your anger stems from, you might find similarities in your career, your hobbies, or even a particular event that irritates you.

GEMINI

You can learn the most about yourself through your social circle, Gemini. It's often said that people with past lives will reconnect in their new lives. If you have a friend or partner that you feel knows you inside and out, a coincidental meeting that led you to your current friend group, or feel a divine connection with someone close to you, you're likely to have known them in your past life, too. Look for connections in your friend group to a certain place, time period, or hobby. This can help you understand which of the people you know may be significantly connected to your past self.

CANCER

You're most likely to pick up hints about your past life from your spirituality, Cancer. That doesn't necessarily mean your past self was religious (although it could) but rather that you connect with them through your own spiritual practices. If there are elements of spirituality that you're particularly drawn to or just find yourself admiring, chances are you were even more devoted to them in a past life. Whether you find yourself enchanted by the idea of practicing witchcraft or just really enjoy relaxing through yoga and meditation, these are good ways to understand your past self and potentially even reconnect with them.

LEO

You'll likely get hints about your past life via your creative hobbies. If there's a type of character you always play, a style of painting you like to make, or songs you love to listen to, these could give you hints about your past self's personality, time period, or region. There could be a particular landscape painting you're always drawn to or a type of music from a specific time period that resonates with you. These can give you the most clues about your past self—when they might have lived, what they were like, or even how they died.

VIRGO

Insights about your past self will come from small facets of your personality. Your sign is all about attention to detail, so it's no surprise that your past self will become most apparent in the little things. Look for unique things about you that people always comment on—the weird, the quirky, the uncommon. Pet peeves, methods of organizing, or even specific strategies you use to remember things could all give you insights into your past self's behavior. You might try to compare these parts of your personality to common jobs or time period traits to learn more about your past life.

LIBRA

You can learn the most about your past self through your morals. Where do you get your values from, and is there any hill you'd die on that's extremely specific to you? Not every Libra was a judge in their past life—although you may certainly act like one—so look for specifics about yourself that could point toward your past self being involved in a certain religion, working a job that was very strict, or advocating for justice during a historic period. The modern issues you fight for could be inspired by a past self who was dedicated to the same kinds of justice.

SCORPIO

Scorpio, your sign often comes with a fascination with the macabre. If you find yourself obsessed with death, spirits, or an afterlife, it's highly likely that you died in a traumatic way in your past life. These lingering questions and obsessions often come from individuals who weren't able to come to terms with their own death in a past life. You might even be able to pick up more hints about your past life if you have a particular fascination: true crime, mysteries, sudden disappearances…

SAGITTARIUS

You can learn most about your past self by examining the types of adventures you enjoy most. If you always yearn for freedom no matter what and will chase it anywhere, chances are your past self was always stuck at home, feeling confined and unable to adventure as they pleased. If you feel more at ease with yourself and drawn to a particular adventure, though, that may say more about your past self's profession or hobby. Natural inclinations towards certain terrains (forests, deserts, water), animals, or activities can give you more insights into what your past self did for work and what they were like.

AQUARIUS

Your sign is a forward-thinker, so to look into your past life, you'll need to examine your own work. Aquarians are known for their innovations, but these commonly use modern technology with futuristic advancements in mind. But that doesn't mean you can't receive a few hints about your past self by looking through your own work. You're likely to be most connected to your past self through your profession, so you may be able to narrow down a few things about who you were and what jobs you might have had. You may also notice that elements of your work or futuristic design is actually inspired by or linked to the past. If you have a specific fascination around one innovation, chances are you've worked with it in the past or your past self lived through the time of its creation.

CAPRICORN

You can gain a lot of insight about your past self by flipping through your goals and achievements. You, Capricorn, will need to look past your profession and hobbies—you're likely to find the most connection to your past self through your deepest desires. There's likely something that you truly yearn for (or maybe have already accomplished) that you feel will bring you deep satisfaction. Maybe most of your goals are centered around that one thing—if it's financial stability, for example, you may have professional, personal, and organizational goals that revolve around money. This goal will not only be something your past self aimed for and desired for themselves, but could represent something they lacked or never achieved in their own life. This manifests itself in your life as a desire to complete something your past self never could.

PISCES

Your sign is unique in that you can often pick up hints about your past life from your dreams. This might not be surprising to you, as you may have already learned about your past self from your subconscious. It's easy for your subconscious mind to pick up on hints and similarities between you and your past life—but keep in mind that these won't appear to you clearly in most cases. Look out for recurring dreams, especially about certain events that you haven't experienced. If you have a regular nightmare about a particular fear or accident, always find yourself in the same landscape during your dream, or have dream people that you constantly meet, these could be relics from your past life visiting you in your sleep.

THE CRYSTAL THAT UNLOCKS YOUR ZODIAC'S DEEPEST INTUITION

ARIES

Aries, the crystal that resonates most with your energy is Carnelian. Known for its vibrant orange hue, Carnelian can help to boost your natural enthusiasm and leadership skills. It's a stone of motivation, endurance, and courage; all of which align perfectly with your ambitious nature.

Carnelian also promotes a sense of calm, which can be helpful when you're dealing with the frustrations that can arise from any obstacles in your path. Keeping this stone close will help to maintain your energy while also promoting patience (a trait that isn't always easy for Aries to master!).

WHAT KIND OF CARNELIAN TO GET:

Aries, a Carnelian necklace will suit you best. It's ideal for you to keep the chain short, so that the Carnelian stone can rest in the hollow of your collarbone. Placing the stone here will help your leadership, communication, and creative expression; all associated with both the Carnelian stone and the placement of this stone over the throat.

TAURUS

Taurus, your earthy nature connects deeply with Rose Quartz, a stone of unconditional love and beauty. Rose Quartz is aligned with your ruling planet, Venus, and will encourage love, compassion, and forgiveness.

Rose Quartz can also aid in creating a peaceful and harmonious environment, something that you might find valuable. Having this crystal in your space will help you to embrace your love for all things beautiful, while also promoting stability, self-care, and tranquility.

WHAT KIND OF ROSE QUARTZ TO GET:

You should buy a Rose Quartz obelisk to display in a room you feel the most comfortable in, such as your bedroom or living room. This shape of crystal is known for spreading its energy throughout a room via the top of the obelisk.

GEMINI

Gemini, your sign is ruled by Mercury, making you the communicator of the zodiac. The crystal that aligns with your sign is Aquamarine. This beautiful ocean-colored stone can help to clear your mind and enhance your communication skills.

Aquamarine resonates with your Gemini energy, as it promotes the flow of ideas and encourages intellectual growth. Keeping this stone nearby can aid you in articulating your thoughts more effectively and encourages intellectual growth: a must for your ever-curious nature.

WHAT KIND OF AQUAMARINE TO GET:

A heart Aquamarine crystal might be appealing to you, Gemini. The heart shape of the stone can help reduce stress and foster positive emotions. It may also have a good influence on your social relationships.

CANCER

Cancer, as a deeply intuitive and emotional water sign, you resonate most with Moonstone. As the name implies, this crystal is closely tied to the Moon, which rules your celestial body. Moonstone enhances your intuitive abilities and helps to balance your emotional state.

It's a stone that can offer you comfort and guide you through the fluctuating tides of your feelings. Having Moonstone nearby can remind you of the cyclical nature of life and that, just like the moon phases, emotions wax and wane; and that's perfectly okay.

WHAT KIND OF MOONSTONE TO GET:

Cancer, you should have a Moonstone necklace on hand. The best necklace for this stone is one that allows it to lay close to your heart; a long chain and a round or tear-drop shaped Moonstone will work best.

LEO

Leo, your sunny and charismatic personality aligns with the golden sparkle of Pyrite. This stone, often called "Fool's Gold," is known for its protective and shielding energy. Don't worry, Leo, you're no fool yourself; Pyrite is a good crystal for your sign because it can boost your self-confidence and stimulate the flow of creative ideas.

Pyrite is also a symbol of prosperity and good luck. Having this stone nearby can support your natural leadership abilities and your desire for recognition. It'll inspire you to work hard and will help you reap the rewards, too.

WHAT KIND OF PYRITE TO GET:

Leo, you should think about purchasing Pyrite earrings or a bracelet. Both will allow you to wear Pyrite while you work and take it with you on days where you need a little extra luck. Plus, Pyrite will be a unique piece to add to your jewelry box.

VIRGO

Virgo, the crystal that suits you best is Amazonite. This soothing turquoise-green stone helps to calm the mind and aids in manifesting your intentions, fitting in with your practical and methodical approach to life.

Amazonite also promotes clear and sincere communication, which can help you articulate your thoughts and feelings more effectively. Keeping this stone close, Virgo, can assist you in finding balance between your heart and mind, supporting your constant search for order.

WHAT KIND OF AMAZONITE TO GET:

Virgo, you might benefit from an Amazonite worry stone. Worry stones are small, smooth stones designed to be carried around everywhere you go; when you're feeling stressed, rubbing your fingers across the cool surface of the stone will help you relax. Amazonite is the perfect material for a beautiful worry stone.

LIBRA

Libra, your sign is all about balance and harmony, making Lepidolite the ideal crystal for you. This stone carries the power of the pink ray, promoting balance, peace, and a sense of calm—attributes that resonate with your sign.

Lepidolite can also assist in decision-making, a process that can sometimes be difficult for your diplomatic self. Having this stone in your vicinity can encourage tranquility and equilibrium, helping to tip the scales in the direction of inner peace.

WHAT KIND OF LEPIDOLITE TO GET:

Libra, you should get a Lepidolite palm stone. Lepidolite is a calming stone; the design of a palm stone, created to fit perfectly in the palm of your hand and provide a grounding weight, matches the energy of Lepidolite well.

SCORPIO

Scorpio, your depth, intensity, and passion work well with the properties of Malachite. Known as the "stone of transformation," Malachite assists in personal growth and healing, qualities that deeply resonate with your Scorpio nature.

Malachite can help to cleanse and purify your energy, encouraging you to break unwanted patterns and habits. Having this crystal nearby can empower you to embrace change and to channel your inner strength, driving you towards continual evolution and self-improvement.

WHAT KIND OF MALACHITE TO GET:

You should definitely consider purchasing polished malachite for display; the inside of this crystal hides unique swirling patterns that can only be seen when cut open. A slice of malachite kept in a space you frequent should bring you the most benefit.

SAGITTARIUS

Sagittarius, your adventurous and philosophical nature is reflected in the properties of the Turquoise stone. Known as a stone of protection, good fortune, and spiritual growth, Turquoise can assist you in your endless search for knowledge and truth.

Turquoise also supports honest communication and self-expression. Carrying this stone with you can encourage a sense of adventure and openness, keeping you true to your free-spirited nature. It may even help you to foster deeper relationships with those around you.

WHAT KIND OF TURQUOISE TO GET:

Sagittarius, you're always on the move. To keep freedom with you wherever you go, consider buying a small pocket stone or getting a turquoise necklace you can wear at all times. This will also make it easy for you to carry Turquoise with you when you travel, where it can help you find new adventures.

CAPRICORN

Capricorn, as an earth sign known for your discipline and determination, the crystal Garnet is a perfect match for you. This deep red stone is known for its grounding energies and for its ability to stimulate focus and perseverance.

Garnet also inspires love and devotion. Keeping this stone close can aid you in your constant pursuit of success while also promoting balance in your relationships and self-care routines. It's a reminder that while you climb to the top, it's also essential to stay grounded and connected to the ones you love.

WHAT KIND OF GARNET TO GET:

Capricorn, Garnet is a stone that you should keep near you. A Garnet ring would benefit your sensible nature while allowing you to wear Garnet at all times. If you're looking for something more low-key, a necklace is also a suitable choice.

AQUARIUS

Aquarius, your innovative and progressive nature aligns with the unique vibrations of Labradorite. Known as the stone of transformation and magic, Labradorite encourages imagination, creativity, and change—qualities that reflect your Aquarian spirit.

Labradorite can also help you to tap into your intuition, enhancing your natural ability to envision possibilities where others can't. Keeping this stone nearby can inspire you, Aquarius, to bring your innovative ideas to life and continue marching to the beat of your own drum.

WHAT KIND OF LABRADORITE TO GET:

Aquarius, you should look for a Labradorite crystal ball. Crystal balls aren't just for seeing into the future; labradorite spheres are believed to help their users reflect on their past while also guiding what they want to happen in their lives. Labradorite is already a stone that will help you realize your goals; pairing this stone with the powerful abilities of a crystal ball is the right move for you.

PISCES

Pisces, your sign is deeply intuitive and emotional, making Amethyst the perfect crystal for you. This purple stone is known for its calming energies and its ability to enhance intuition and spiritual growth.

Amethyst also encourages peace and balance, which can help you navigate the ebb and flow of your emotions.

Keeping this crystal in your space, Pisces, can serve as a constant reminder of your connection to the spiritual realm and your ability to find harmony amidst the chaos. It may also help you relax when placed in a prominent part of a room you spend a lot of time in.

WHAT KIND OF AMETHYST TO GET:

You should look for an Amethyst geode to enjoy the raw beauty of this purple quartz. Geodes are believed to help drive new energies and positivity, and are also well-known stress relievers. An Amethyst geode will bring you new dreams and tranquility.

THE COLOR OF YOUR AURA, BASED ON YOUR ZODIAC SIGN

ARIES: RED

Red auras are known for being passionate and bold. They're also associated with people who are grounded; Aries, you're known for being no-nonsense when it comes to your work and goals, so your sign naturally fits with a red aura color. Plus, red is typically related to high energy levels; seeing as you pretty much never run out of productive energy, Aries, it makes sense that your sign's aura color would be red.

TAURUS: GREEN

Your sign's aura, Taurus, is green; meant to represent people who have a healing aura focused around comfort. Your love of stability and reassurance makes a green aura the greatest fit for your zodiac sign. Green is also often a color that's related to nature and the environment, including signifying a love of the earth or a naturally comforting personality.

GEMINI: YELLOW

Yellow is the most friendly aura color there is, Gemini, signifying someone who is generally down-to-earth and social. Yellow is often deemed a good color to have because it can signify health and confidence; as an easy-going and typically extroverted individual, you naturally fit best with a yellow aura.

CANCER: SILVER

Cancer, silver auras are typically related to empathy, spirituality, and high emotions. Silver is also an aura color commonly associated with the moon, your ruling planet. This aura color signifies your nurturing personality and deep emotional connections with others; it also reflects your natural intuition.

LEO: PURPLE

Leo, purple auras are typically associated with a regal personality—befitting of anyone under the sign of the lion. Purple auras often signify a love of luxury and are often associated with creative signs. They can also represent someone who is imaginative or is generally very social.

VIRGO: BLUE

Blue is a highly logical color, one that signifies knowledge and wisdom. It's also a calm color, which is befitting of your sign, Virgo, since you're rarely stressed and always prepared. Blue is also the color of communication—useful for a sign whose ruling planet is Mercury, the planet of communication.

LIBRA: VIOLET

Libra, violet auras are commonly known to be associated with those who are intelligent and multi-talented. Violet is a color that can represent your social charm and natural grace; violet is often related to being a visionary for the future or easily finding creative inspiration. Your natural people skills and ability to follow through on your goals makes your sign the best match for a violet aura.

SCORPIO: INDIGO

Indigo is typically associated with individuals who are very spiritual; your natural intuition and interest in spirituality give your sign an indigo aura. You have a keen ability to self-reflect and understand your subconscious mind, and you're also highly intuitive; these are all qualities that are also present in individuals with indigo auras.

SAGITTARIUS: ORANGE

Sagittarius, orange is often associated with creative signs who have a lot of energy. Orange is most common in individuals who are highly optimistic, just like your sign—orange is also typically associated with spontaneous adventures and a love of challenges, making it the color that most suits your sign's aura.

CAPRICORN: TAN

Capricorn, tan auras are most commonly associated with those who are dependable and down-to-earth. Your discipline, willpower, and work ethic reflect a tan aura; you're very no-nonsense, but this is your ultimate strength when it comes to achieving your goals.

AQUARIUS: TURQUOISE

Turquoise auras are most often associated with those who are free-willed. Turquoise is also a color associated with knowledge, which suits your sign; additionally, turquoise can relate to good communication. For your sign, Aquarius, turquoise represents your innovation and passion for your work.

PISCES: PINK

Pink is the color of romance and love—when it comes to your sign's aura, Pisces, you're all about the emotional intuition, caring, and hopeless romanticism that comes with a sweet pink aura. You're a sign that's connected with both dreams and reality, making a pink aura most fitting for you.

DIVINE FEMININITY IS COMING IF YOU'VE PULLED THESE TAROT CARDS

THE EMPRESS

The Empress is strongly associated with femininity. She represents fertility, nurturing, and creative pursuits; she is often a symbol of life and motherhood. The Empress represents powerful femininity and strength. For many, she is a sacred card to receive.

The Empress may appear to those who are entering their divine feminine era. She may appear to a querent who has already unlocked their powerful femininity and has realized their capabilities already. She may also be pulled by someone who is creating new artistic and energetic pursuits for themselves.

The Empress is often thought to represent the softer side of divine femininity. Those who are caring, nurturing, look out for others, and are connected and aware in their relationships may feel a deep connection to the Empress card. Additionally, a querent who is highly connected to nature and the world around them may pull the Empress card more regularly or receive her advice in their readings.

THE HIGH PRIESTESS

The High Priestess is another sacred card of divine femininity. The High Priestess represents the spiritual and feeling side of femininity. She is all about listening to your intuition and understanding your feelings. She may bring spiritual guidance to your life or point out areas in which spiritual insight will soon make its way to you.

The High Priestess can also be an illusive card. You may find interpreting her meaning to be frustrating when you pull this card. She can be difficult to understand—and part of that is because she implores you to go with your gut feeling and trust what your intuition is telling you. Many people see her as being positively secretive—she knows the answers you seek, but she wants you to come to your own conclusion instead of telling you outright.

The High Priestess arrives with significant amounts of divine feminine energy that radiate from her presence. She represents divine spirituality, feminine witchcraft, spiritual devotion, and is often seen to be connected to the Moon or the spiritual world. If the Empress card is about being connected to the people and the Earth, then the High Priestess is about being connected to the entire Universe.

Someone who is just coming into their divine femininity or beginning their divine feminine era may pull the High Priestess card. A person who is still learning to trust their intuition or allow themselves to be a leader may hear from the High Priestess often. Additionally, a querent who is embracing their spirituality and learning to trust their practices may receive guidance from the High Priestess as well.

STRENGTH

The Strength card typically depicts a woman standing next to a lion and petting it fondly. The Strength card is divinely feminine; it represents confidence, finding your power, and trusting yourself. The Strength card is less about physical strength and more about mental or inner strength; it may be advising you to stay true to your values and express yourself confidently.

Strength is more often than not said to be about power that does not have to be forced. It is longevity, fortitude, and self-assuredness. It is being calm yet strong in the face of all obstacles. Strength tames the lion not with violence, but with ease and grace. Strength brings about harmony and peace in all things.

If you have been hard at work on your self-esteem, have chosen wisdom and power in your actions, or are facing obstacles with inner strength, you may pull the Strength card. She may also advise you to take the high road, to trust yourself, and to address your daily life with confidence. She may guide you towards embracing your divine femininity and not being ashamed of expressing it. She may also appear to commend you on your inner work and the fact that you have entered your divine feminine era.

YOUR ZODIAC SIGN'S TAROT CARD SUIT, BASED ON YOUR ELEMENT

PENTACLES: EARTH—TAURUS, VIRGO, AND CAPRICORN

Pentacles most commonly represent material possessions. This means that the Pentacles suit may have something to say about your finances, things you own, or even your professional life.

For each Earth sign, finances are known to be your strong suit. This naturally relates your signs' element to the Pentacles cards, which frequently come up in relation to your personal finances or even your finances in relation to your work.

The Pentacles suit can generally be a sign of stability, loyalty, and family—things that all Earth signs value deeply, to the point where these values become key traits of each Earth zodiac sign.

When it comes to relationships, the Pentacles suit recognizes slow growth and movement towards security and stability—though it can also be a sign that your relationship needs some excitement. This may be true for all Earth signs; being grounded, responsible, and reliable are all known traits of Earth zodiac signs, although they may also struggle with igniting passion and excitement into their lives at times. Taurus tends to become too comfortable in their comfort zone, Virgo goes slowly for fear of not being perfect, and Capricorn is often stoic. The Pentacles suit can relate to all of these things, although they are generally viewed as a welcome tarot card to receive thanks to their stable natures.

SWORDS: AIR—GEMINI, LIBRA, AND AQUARIUS

The Swords suit is usually known for representing intellect. Swords often represent logic over emotion, though they can also represent anxiety and even conflict. The Swords suit can either be positive, bringing energetic change and power, or negative, representing swift anger or even misfortune.

Each Air sign of the zodiac is known for being highly intellectual and logical. However, Air signs can sometimes be seen as fickle or known for having some pitfalls when it comes to their logic and ruthless determination. Libra struggles to set boundaries, Gemini finds it difficult to follow through on things, and Aquarius struggles with tradition and lack of constant change.

All Air zodiac signs are highly analytical and known to be good at communication. Gemini is ruled by Mercury, the planet of communication, Libra is recognized as the zodiac's best mediator, and Aquarius enjoys workshopping their innovations with others. Each Air zodiac sign is generally very social—especially thanks to their high levels of communication.

The Swords suit often provides paths to resolving issues of the mind. The Swords frequently deal with conflict and may bring warnings or messages related to these issues.

CUPS: WATER—CANCER, SCORPIO, AND PISCES

The Cups suit deals with emotional situations—not surprising for water signs that are all highly intuitive and in-tune with their own feelings. Cancer and Pisces especially are known for being sensitive, empathetic signs that feel others' feelings almost as if they were their own. Scorpio is an incredibly intuitive sign that connects with people deeply on an emotional level. It's no surprise that the element of water binds these three signs with Cups.

Cups can have emotional meaning relating to love, relationships, and feelings. The Cups suit can also relate to spirituality, perfect for signs like Cancer who are already associated with being spiritual.

Cups is also a highly imaginative suit, sometimes even dealing with dreams—matching with signs like Pisces, thanks to their inherent romanticism and imagination. This also helps the suit relate well to Scorpio, the most intuitive water sign.

Cups cards tend to also represent things like creativity and self-expression. With each water sign in the zodiac harnessing a different creative facet and displaying varied creative interests, they make up different aspects of the Cups suit.

Interestingly, because of their emotional capacity and intuition, the water signs of the zodiac are often highly proficient at reading tarot cards. This makes them better at understanding and following the meanings and warnings of tarot cards in their own life, as well as helping others do the same when it comes to their readings.

WANDS: FIRE—ARIES, LEO, AND SAGITTARIUS

Wands often deal with facets of creativity, strength, and passion. The suit of Wands is sometimes referred to as the suit of Sticks—one idea behind their design—because they are a foundational creation of the tarot deck. They are often seen as spiritual and can relate to the growth, passion, and drive of an individual.

It's no surprise that this intense suit relates to the fire signs of the zodiac. Each of these signs devote themselves to passion and self-expression in their own unique way. Aries is headstrong and ambitious, Leo is the center of attention and highly creative, and Sagittarius is endlessly adventurous and determined. Each of these signs' passions for their interests, professional lives, and values is a key part of their personality, making them deeply affixed to the suit of Wands.

Many times, Wands signify taking action. Sometimes, this action can be destructive, but will lead to new growth and ambition in the future. Sometimes, this action is in pursuit of a sudden spark, of passion, of romance, and of the desire to achieve.

The fire signs of the zodiac will often find themselves acting spontaneously out of instinct or drive. They seek out the spark in life and create changes for themselves that are deeply inspired and meaningful. Sometimes, as the suit of Wands can also warn against, these signs can become egotistical or place too much weight on success and power. The negative side of the Wands can also indicate a lack of ambition or having no sense of purpose.

Fire signs are often impressive because of their dedication and determination. Their passion can sometimes be a wildfire, but like the suit of Wands, often signifies positive changes, new growth, and a deep love of and connection to a meaningful life.

3 ZODIAC SIGNS WHO MAKE THE BEST TAROT CARD READERS

SCORPIO

It's no surprise that Scorpios are often considered rulers of the tarot card deck. You have a deep sense of self and an ability to read other people that often surprises those around you. Your connection with your own intuition (and those of others) makes you an uncannily good tarot card reader. If you've noticed that people often come to you for advice on something you shouldn't be able to predict, this might be a further sign that reading tarot cards could net you some solid ideas about the paths you and your loved ones should take in the future.

PISCES

You're known for your imagination and intuition, Pisces. You're also often known to be a spiritual sign, or at least are good at engaging in spiritual practices—think journaling and meditation. You're also good at connecting things together in your mind, creating stories and meanings from the cards that you draw. This can make you a vivid tarot card reader, helping others understand what their cards mean for their personal life and the steps they should take in the future. Guided by your never-ending creativity and intuition, you're likely to make a highly proficient tarot card reader.

CANCER

Thanks to your natural sense of empathy and deep spirituality, tarot cards might just be for you. Your ruling planet, the moon, is often associated with spirituality and spiritual practices. This could make you highly proficient when it comes to practicing with tarot cards, giving you a leg up when it comes to reading and understanding them. Your empathy and caring nature when it comes to others can help them benefit the most from your readings, allowing you to guide them both in understanding what their cards mean and how they can take action for their own futures.

THESE 3 ZODIAC SIGNS ARE UNUSUALLY CONNECTED TO THE ELEMENTS

CANCER

You have several factors that make you a highly elemental zodiac sign, Cancer. As a water sign, you may feel naturally soothed by bodies of water; this also contributes to your serene attitude. You're also a highly sensitive and empathetic sign, which can help you to feel more in tune with nature—especially animals—in general. Plus, your ruling planet is the Moon. Not only does this improve your interactions with water and even wind, it also changes your energies alongside the Moon's cycle, leaving you extraordinarily connected to the elements.

TAURUS

You're an earth sign, Taurus, but your sign tends to be especially connected to nature. Not only are you a grounded, responsible person, you also tend to feel more at peace when you're surrounded by greenery or isolated in nature. Your sign is likely to have a green thumb and be interested in gardening or tending indoor plants. You tend to prefer a generally quiet and calm life, which contributes to your ability to attract nature as much as it attracts you.

SAGITTARIUS

You're a fire sign, which you may or may not feel deeply connected to depending on your personality. Fire may not soothe or calm you in the way that other elements do for other signs. But that doesn't mean you're not generally connected to the elements. Not only do you enjoy being outdoors—immersing yourself in the natural world around you—but your sign also tends to be an explorer, enjoying finding all the hidden beauty the world has to offer. This kind of exploration often attracts closeness and connection with all of the elements. It also reconnects you with your sign's element, giving you the same passion and long-burning life flame that fire itself represents.

APOLLO'S TAROT CARDS CAN GUIDE YOUR INTUITION TO NEW HEIGHTS

Apollo, the god of prophecy and foresight, was known for bestowing prophetic powers upon his oracles. Just as he had the gift of predicting the future, many tarot cards are related to Apollo directly. They may not allow you to see the future, but they can bring new intuitive meaning to your life when you receive them.

THE MAGICIAN

The Magician is a card that is directly connected to Apollo himself, thought to represent him specifically. When you receive this card, it means that you have complete control over yourself and your life. The Magician is a sign that you have achieved success; that you feel confident and powerful; that you have the tools you need to feel complete.

The Magician is seen by many as a card that can also be about manifesting. You have all you need to fulfill your ambitions, so now it is up to you to utilize your determination and manifest your truest desires. Apollo himself brings confidence, creativity, and complete truth in all things. He is often also related to the concept of purifying; if you have faced many obstacles lately and found growth and rebirth after them, Apollo may be guiding your way.

The Magician is a sign to trust your intuition and use your present skills to achieve your goals. The Magician appears when you are confident and on the right path; when your intuition is loud and clear, when you have an undoubted vision and the confidence to follow it completely.

THE CHARIOT

If you have been facing many challenges lately but have conquered them all—or are devising new ways to solve the problems you've been faced with—then the Chariot may appear to you. This card is not directly related to Apollo like the Magician is, but it is thought by many to be one of Apollo's cards because of the presence of the Chariot in both the Major Arcana and as the vehicle Apollo himself drives.

The Chariot represents inner strength. If you trust your intuition and allow it to guide you, you will overcome all of the challenges you face. You need only rely on your own wit and determination to succeed. Your gut feelings will lead the way in overcoming any obstacle you are presented with. Apollo's confidence, spirit, and mastery connects to the Chariot when they both ask you to trust yourself and move forward according to what you feel is right.

THE SUN

The Sun is another card that is often thought to be related to Apollo because he is associated with the Sun. Apollo brings with him all the qualities of the Sun, as does the Sun tarot card; it means high spirits, joy and playfulness, and success. It brings new life and new energy. The Sun may appear when you have been trusting your innermost thoughts and healing your subconscious mind; it tells you that you are on the right path. It may appear when you have achieved something recently or on the path to achieving a goal.

Like Apollo himself, the Sun asks you to celebrate yourself and your intuitive mind. It wants you to trust that you have the power to achieve your goals and bring yourself to a higher state of being; that you can succeed by following your own innate drive.

ARTEMIS'S TAROT CARDS WILL GUIDE YOUR DIVINE FEMININE ERA

Artemis, the goddess of the Moon, the wilderness, and protector of women, is known for being a highly spiritual and sacred figure. She is often the head of divine femininity, as she carries herself with ultimate strength and power and is known for using her powers to protect women in need of help. If you are entering your divine feminine era or uncovering your own inner strength, you may look to Artemis to guide you. These tarot cards—which are highly related to the goddess herself—may help light your way to your new chapter.

THE MOON

The Moon arrives to unveil the secrets hidden within you. This card is said to deal with the subconscious mind; it wants to unveil your fears, your secrets, and your hidden shadow self. These are the things you must confront in order to move forward; by exposing them, the Moon brings about healing.

The Moon is often associated with spirituality because of the meaning of our Moon itself. Long associated with Artemis, the Moon symbolizes nature, spirituality, healing, and new energy. As goddess of the Moon, when you pull the Moon card, you may be receiving guidance from Artemis herself.

In order to move into your divine feminine era—of which Artemis would most certainly be approving—you must work on healing your past self. You cannot reach your highest self without working on who you are currently. The Moon aims to bring these two selves into harmony by forcing you to begin your divine healing journey.

THE HIGH PRIESTESS

The High Priestess is often said to be the most powerful feminine card in the entire tarot. She is often known to be sacred and divine. She is highly spiritual and mysterious, and is believed to be deeply connected with the Moon.

Artemis is associated with both the Moon and with priestesses, and is a protector of women. The High Priestess is intrinsically connected with this Greek goddess through her spirituality, intuition, and communes with the subconscious.

If you receive the High Priestess in a reading, know that you must trust your intuition and your subconscious. The solutions you seek are already within you; listen to your heart and your gut, and you'll know what to do. Clarity will soon come to you, but you must uncover it for yourself.

THE EMPRESS

The Empress is about nurturing and caring. She has connections to Artemis—both figures rule over fertility and are known to protect women or be hallmarks of femininity. The Empress sparks creativity in all who receive her, breathing new life into old projects or giving a querent a new idea to inspire them.

Both Artemis and the Empress are protectors, relating them to one another. The two women are known to be nurturing and caring, especially for those close to them. They imbue that spirit into those who follow them and look for their guidance; if you want to care for your loved ones, are protective of those close to you, or show your love to those you care for deeply, then both the Empress card and Artemis may appear to guide you.

HERE'S HOW TO CLEANSE YOUR TAROT CARDS

Tarot is a practice everyone can enjoy, whether or not you're spiritual. If you want to get the most out of your cards energetically, you may choose to cleanse your tarot cards every once in a while. This isn't at all a necessary practice when it comes to practicing tarot, so you should only do it if you feel it would help you connect more closely with your tarot cards.

A few times in which you might choose to clean your tarot cards could be after someone else has used them, during a full moon, after they have reached a certain number of uses, or when you feel disconnected from your cards.

Certain cleansing practices are considered 'closed' practices, which means that they are culturally or spiritually significant, and you shouldn't practice them if you don't belong to the closed practice. However, tarot itself is an open practice—anyone can do it—and there are plenty of ways to clean your tarot cards that you can complete no matter what the tarot cards mean to you.

SAY A MANTRA WHILE SHUFFLING THE DECK

You may choose to reset your tarot deck by stating your intentions while reshuffling it. Touch each of the cards and repeat an affirmation, say a personal mantra, or simply think or speak about cleansing the deck as you shuffle it.

Do this when you feel full of positive energy and hope. Imbue your energy and state of mind into the cards as you shuffle or touch each one of them. Imagine all of the negative energy leaving the cards as you cleanse them with your positive energy.

BURN A CANDLE OR INCENSE

If you have a favorite candle or type of incense that smells good to you, you may want to burn it in order to cleanse your tarot cards. Smoke cleansing is an open practice and is perfectly appropriate for you; it usually involves burning incense, herbs, or a candle, and steering the smoke towards the cards, leaving the cards in an enclosed space with the smoke, or fanning the smoke over both sides of the tarot cards.

Be careful with this method, as you don't want to get soot on your tarot deck. Note that you are practicing smoke cleansing, not smudging—and if you're planning on burning herbs, never use white sage. Both of these things are closed practices, whereas smoke cleansing is an open one!

LEAVE THE DECK UNDER THE LIGHT OF THE MOON

The moon is known to recharge energy, and you might have heard of many people leaving their crystals out under a full moon to recharge. You can do the same thing with your tarot deck. A full moon is usually best because it signifies new beginnings, new energy, and is considered to be most powerful. But you can leave your tarot deck under any kind of moonlight if you need an emergency cleansing.

If you choose to cleanse your tarot deck this way, you may decide to leave your tarot cards out under the light of the moon every cycle of the full moon. You might also opt for leaving it out during astrological events like a harvest moon, a blue moon, or a strawberry moon; this can imbue even more energy into your deck and prepare it for the season ahead.

You can leave your tarot cards outside under the light of the moon as long as they're in a safe place, but this isn't necessary. Your cards can receive all the light they need from inside the home as long as they're in an area that receives moonlight.

THIS IS WHAT IT MEANS WHEN YOU PULL THE SAME TAROT CARD OVER AND OVER

Have you ever noticed that a tarot card seems to be 'following' you when you do readings? Maybe there's a card that you can't stop pulling, or one that stands out to you more than the rest. If you're having trouble figuring out why this card keeps coming to you, there are a few reasons you might be pulling the same card again…and again…and again.

YOU HAVEN'T LEARNED ITS LESSON

One clear reason for a tarot card to consistently reappear is if you're ignoring it or misinterpreting it. Tarot cards appear to offer you advice; they allow you to make positive changes regarding your present situations. Sometimes they tell you you're on the right path—other times there are things they want you to work on or change. The tricky part about all this is that there are many different interpretations for each card; you might think a card is warning you about your finances when really it wants you to pay attention to your relationship, or maybe you're trying to ignore a card you think is a bad omen when really it's just telling you to do some shadow work.

If you've been receiving a tarot card frequently, you should think up every possible meaning you can interpret from it in one session. Ask clarifying questions to see what it might mean; you can pull additional cards to try to understand what the original card is telling you. There may be multiple areas of your life where this card applies; if that's the case, you may want to work on all of those areas and see if the card agrees with your work.

IT'S CLOSELY CONNECTED TO YOU

Receiving the same card over and over again isn't usually a bad sign. It might just mean that you're closely connected to the tarot card in some way.

Is the tarot card you're pulling frequently actually your birth tarot card? Does it relate to your zodiac sign or your sun sign's element? What about your ruling planet? Does it mean something to you symbolically or emotionally—for example, do you feel hopeful each time you see the Star card, or are you a spiritual person who adores the Moon?

These tarot cards can sometimes have personal meanings rather than exclusively what is on the card. Sometimes, people will find individual meanings within cards that appear frequently to them—especially if they are their birth card or significant to them in some other way. If this is the case, a tarot card may merely be reappearing to you to signify positivity, hopefulness, reassurance, faith, guidance, or just that you're doing something right. You can consider these cards like guardian angels, appearing to you when you need them.

YOU FEAR IT

This might sound strange, but if there are certain tarot cards that you're afraid to receive, you might notice them more than often. Your energy can affect the deck, and your inner fear of receiving a particular card might actually be saying that there's something within yourself that you're scared of working on. In that case, of course the tarot deck will want to present you with that card more and more often—it wants to guide you.

Some tarot cards that are sometimes negatively perceived by many can include cards like Death, the Devil, or the Ten of Swords. The more you resist a certain card, the more you may unintentionally attract it.

But there are many meanings to any tarot card. Death can represent positive changes and new beginnings. The Devil can represent self-care and indulgence. The Ten of Swords can be about accepting major life changes. A tarot card may not be reappearing to you to constantly signify something negative; if you believe this to be true, you may just be struggling with confirmation bias. Look for a different meaning when this card reappears to you. Is there emotional work you can be doing? Inner reflections you've been grappling with? Something in your life you genuinely want to change? Take these kinds of cards as signs that hard work creates the ultimate positive change. When you learn to understand and apply them rather than fear them, you probably won't pull them as often.

THESE 4 ZODIAC SIGNS NEED TO RECONNECT WITH THEIR DIVINE INNER SELF

SAGITTARIUS

Now is a good time for you to engage in some introspection, Sagittarius. You need to rework some of your routines and go-to activities to better suit you. If you've been feeling unmotivated or uninspired lately, it's likely because you're feeling a little lost and unbalanced when it comes to your inner self. You might struggle to recognize what you need or feel disconnected from some of the passions that usually drive you.

To help with this, you may want to consider trying as many new things as possible this month. Test out various routines and see if any of them spark inspiration in you. Try new physical activities, new hobbies, and new ways of working. Mix up your daily schedule and see if it makes you more productive. This month is about spending time with yourself, understanding what you really want, and marking the growth you've had throughout the past year with a transformed routine for yourself.

ARIES

Aries, you need to spend time reconnecting with yourself lately. If you've been feeling disjointed or uncertain about your future goals, it's probably because you've lost sight of what you really want in life. This may be because your passions and interests have changed or just because you haven't been reflecting enough lately.

For your sign, physical activity often works best as a way for you to expend your pent-up energy and help your mind focus and be brought into a meditative state. This is how you truly clear up all your confusing thoughts and uncertainties; by dedicating time to cleanse your inner self and reconnect with your ambitions. Not only does this have the benefit of helping you relax, feel refreshed, and prevent burnout, it will also help you better understand what you want to focus on in your personal and professional life.

CAPRICORN

You need to focus on self-healing and resolution, Capricorn. You have a good handle on your inner desires and long-term goals, but that doesn't mean there aren't parts of your inner self that aren't being addressed. Now is a good time for you to recognize these parts and work with them to reach a new understanding of yourself and your subconscious.

Whether you want to focus on healing past issues that haven't been addressed, looking into root causes of anxieties and fears, or spend time learning to better understand your subconscious, you'll find that taking the time to work with your inner self can provide you with a healthier, more holistic day-to-day outlook. You might find yourself feeling more productive, less anxious, and even sleeping better at night once you begin to address your divine inner self.

LIBRA

You might benefit from meditations and reflections that center around your past, focusing on your personal growth and any issues that are still bothering you. As a sign who struggles with conflict resolution, this can often pertain to your inner self, too.

You may accidentally disconnect from parts of you that you feel didn't perform well under pressure or are connected to memories you don't want to remember. This makes you incredibly good at compartmentalizing, but this can also be an issue when it comes to working with the full inner self.

To address this, journaling and meditation can help you. You might want to write out a full timeline of your life or of events you want to address to see where you want to focus. You can reflect on specific memories, on your recent growth, or on a longer period of time. This will help you align your past self with your present self, providing you access to the full version of your inner self.

HERE'S HOW TO FIND YOUR TAROT BIRTH CARD

Did you know that, according to numerology, everyone has a guiding tarot card? You can find it using your birthday—and you'll often find that using this tarot card to give you additional insights into your personal life and personality can be extremely insightful. You can also couple your tarot birth card with your astrological chart; this can give you detailed information about your true self.

Finding your birth tarot card is simple. It is guaranteed to be in the Major Arcana: the twenty-two cards in the tarot deck that are named.

You'll first use numerology to calculate your birth number. First, add up all of the numbers in your birthday together. If you were born on December 7th, 1999, you would calculate: 12 + 7 + 1 + 9 + 9 + 9, which equals 47.

But you'll need to continue a little further to get your actual numerology 'life path' number. You should also add 4 + 7 to get 11. This is because, in numerology, birth numbers are supposed to be single digit—except when you receive the numbers 11, 22, or 33.

For calculating your birth tarot card, however, you can simply reduce your birthday until you reach a number within the Major Arcana. The Major Arcana has 22 cards, all of which are numbered (sometimes excluding the Fool).

Continuing with the above example, if you were to receive 11 as your reduced number, your birth tarot card would be Justice.

If you continue following numerology in this manner, you can find even more guidance within the tarot deck. Some prefer to pull directly from the date of their birth if it is already single-digit. Some choose to add only the two digits of their birth date together, while others will add the month as well. Depending on the results you get from the numbers that are important to you, there could be several tarot cards that speak to you and your personality.

Once you have uncovered your birth tarot card, look out for it. It may be a card that frequently appears to you, or it may have special meaning when you do pull it in your readings.

It can be useful to recognize your birth tarot card—when it appears, it is likely that the deck is trying to give you a meaningful message. Knowing that a tarot card is your birth card could change your interpretation of the deck's guidance slightly.

THESE CRYSTALS ARE PERFECT FOR READING TAROT CARDS

Crystals aren't necessary to help you read tarot cards, but if you enjoy using them, you might be pleased to know that the two can intersect. There are many ways you can use crystals to help you with your tarot readings—whether you choose to use them to cleanse your cards, charge your cards with new energy, or place them during the readings to help you interpret what your tarot deck is saying.

No matter what you choose to do with your crystals, you should know of a few common crystals that can help you during your tarot readings.

CLEAR QUARTZ

Used to connect your energy more deeply with the tarot deck and invite the cards to answer you, clear quartz might enhance the effectiveness of your readings. If you struggle to interpret the cards in front of you or feel like your energy when reading is off, clear quartz can help you enhance your emotions and make things crystal clear to your tarot deck.

ROSE QUARTZ

If you're planning on doing a love reading with your tarot cards, you might want to use rose quartz. Commonly known to represent romance and true love, this crystal can help you manifest your romantic desires and set your intentions before you begin your tarot reading.

BLACK TOURMALINE

This crystal is known to help its users focus and feel more protected. It can dispel momentary anxieties and may help you focus more deeply on your tarot deck while reading. This can also help you interpret the cards more clearly; black tourmaline may help prevent you from becoming overly clouded by your own fears or emotions. It is also known to be protective.

AMETHYST

Amethyst is well-known for being a protective crystal. It can protect the energy of both you and your tarot deck while you read. It is also a healing crystal that may make your readings more powerful. Amethyst is also fantastic for clearing negative energy, which may help to cleanse your tarot deck occasionally if you feel it needs it.

CITRINE

Energizing and giving positivity to its owners, citrine can be a great crystal to ward off the frustrations that may come with interpreting your tarot readings. It can help to moderate the energies exchanging between you and your tarot deck, and will revitalize both you and the deck during and in between tarot readings.

SELENITE

Selenite is said to bestow peace and mental wellbeing upon its users. Selenite will help to cleanse your deck of negative energy and can give you something to focus on during a reading. It will give you positivity and renewed energy during your readings, and can also help you calm down before a reading to ensure that you are in the right state of mind to interpret the cards you pull.

LABRADORITE

This crystal can protect against negative energies, which can help cleanse your tarot deck and help protect your energy while you read. Additionally, labradorite is known to help you connect more deeply with your inner self and intuition. Tarot is deeply connected to the subconscious mind, so this crystal may help you interpret tarot's meaning if it is not related to your conscious self.

HOW TO CHOOSE A TAROT DECK THAT SPEAKS TO YOU

Wondering where to turn to for your next tarot deck? The deck you choose can change the way you interact with and even interpret the cards you pull.

TRADITIONAL VS. NON-TRADITIONAL DECKS

Some artists will choose to add new cards with different meanings to their tarot decks. Others may rename certain suits or cards to fit the artistic style of the deck they're trying to create. There's absolutely nothing wrong with doing this; after all, renamed tarot cards will still hold the same meaning as their original counterparts.

When choosing a tarot deck, it's important to consider whether or not you want a deck that remains completely traditional to the Rider-Waite-Smith tarot deck—or if you care at all. If you're serious about wanting a deck that contains only tarot cards with their original names, it'll certainly be easy to find. Just make sure that you're purchasing from an artist who stays true to the original names of each suit.

EXAMINE THE ILLUSTRATIONS

Are you looking for a tarot deck that's modern? Artistic? Traditional? Inspired by something specific—like astronomy or witches? Geared towards a certain kind of person?

You should take your time when selecting a tarot deck and carefully examine the art of as many cards as possible. Keep in mind that there's nothing wrong with picking a deck that matches your personal aesthetic or even the style of your home—if you want to use it regularly and display it, it's important that you choose a deck that you like looking at. You can even opt for completely nontraditional tarot decks like ones that are highly futuristic or minimalist.

When you appreciate the art and design of a tarot deck, you're more likely to use it (and display it). As long as you like the style of tarot deck you choose, you'll be able to interpret the cards more easily and will apply them to your situation more frequently—a double win.

KNOW THE SELLER

It's always best to buy tarot cards that have been designed by an artist or writer—and it's even better to purchase them from a bookstore or local retailer. This will ensure that you're receiving original, high-quality cards. Believe it or not, counterfeit tarot cards are a real issue. Not only will these have plenty of errors and mistakes that could affect your reading, they also steal work from the original artist.

In order to ensure the deck of tarot cards you're purchasing will truly work, make sure you're purchasing an original deck of tarot cards—not a counterfeit product.

FEEL THE CARDS

You can definitely buy tarot cards online—and might actually find a wider selection of cards by doing so—but there's nothing wrong with actually touching the cards once you receive them and making sure you can connect with the deck. Does it feel like the deck speaks to you? Do you feel able to ask the deck questions? Are the images and words clear?

Once you've made contact with the deck, you'll likely feel that it has more personal importance to you. This can help make tarot readings an intentional practice; one that calms and guides you.

WANT TO READ TAROT FOR SOMEONE? HERE ARE 6 TIPS

If you're getting into tarot and want to try giving someone else a reading, there are a few ways you might choose to do so. It's all up to personal preference when it comes to how you give others a tarot reading, so here are some ideas to get you started.

CHOOSE A SPECIFIC DIRECTION TO READ THE CARDS

Some readers prefer to draw the cards so that they face their querent. Others will draw the cards and set them down facing themselves. The most important part is to make sure you choose a direction in which you want to read the tarot. This is because you need to know which way is 'right side up' in order to properly read card reversals. This is all based on personal preference, so you can let the querent know that you'll be displaying the cards towards them so they can see them first, or that since you'll be the one reading their cards, you will have them facing towards you.

YOUR QUERENT DOESN'T NEED TO HAVE A QUESTION

Whether or not you want your querent to have a specific question in mind for their reading is up to both you and them. If they have something they want answered, they should let you know what it is. This way, you will be able to interpret the reading appropriately in terms of their question. This will also ensure that you are able to address the deck with their situation in mind, which is especially important if you're pulling the cards yourself.

But if your querent wants advice on a situation or on their life generally, they don't need to have a specific question in mind. If they prefer to remain more private about their reading, you can even offer to pull cards for them and describe a few situations they might apply to so that your querent can connect the dots themselves. Your goal is to help the querent pull the cards and then understand their meaning, so whatever way the two of you choose to do this is acceptable.

LET THE QUERENT PICK THE CARDS

If you're planning on helping someone else read their tarot cards, you might want to allow them to pick out their cards themselves. This often feels more intentional for the querent and gives them a chance to connect with the cards on their own. Especially if your querent has a lot of specific emotional energy around their reading, they may be able to select cards that apply to their situation accurately—even if they've never done a tarot reading before.

OR, PICK THE CARDS YOURSELF

Some tarot readers believe that other people should not touch their tarot deck. This is because everyone has a different energy they bring to a tarot reading. If you value energy when performing readings and believe that your tarot deck will respond best to only your energy, then you may decide that you do not want any other querent to touch your cards. This is perfectly acceptable; you can perform a tarot reading for someone else without having them touch your cards at all. Just let your querent know that you'll be picking and reading the cards for them.

DON'T TRY TO PREDICT SOMEONE'S FUTURE

Generally, tarot cards are not meant to predict anyone's future. They merely look at the situation a person is currently in and address potential outcomes of that situation. This means that you should not attempt to convince your querent that something specific is going to happen to them in the future. Remind your querent that tarot cards do not remove the querent's free will; instead, they guide the querent to making wise decisions about their life. They can help the querent to address problems in their life they are unaware of, subconsciously avoiding, or do not know how to face. But you cannot predict someone else's future with a deck of tarot cards.

FEEL FREE TO SAY NO

Setting boundaries when reading tarot can be difficult to do. You might feel pressured into giving a reading to someone. You may feel bad saying no if a person is asking for continuous readings or if they want a long, in-depth reading. You might even decide that a question a querent is asking is not appropriate for you or the cards to answer. These are your choices to make. When in doubt, it's always best to conserve the energy and the energy of your cards. Feel free to decline a reading for any reason—and you can also let your querent know when you don't want to answer a question they have.

When giving someone a tarot reading, you might want to consider rules and boundaries you want to establish beforehand. This isn't always necessary for casual readings, especially when you trust the querent and have a good relationship with them. But if there's anything specific you don't want to address or anything the querent should (or shouldn't) do to make you more comfortable as the reader, let them know before your session begins. This will make it easier to enforce those boundaries later on.

IS THERE A SPECIFIC TIME OF DAY YOU SHOULD READ TAROT? MAYBE—HERE'S WHEN

The time of day you'll want to read your tarot cards can depend on the person. This is because your tarot reading can fluctuate with your energy—which is just one reason why most people recommend avoiding reading tarot cards when you're stressed, angry, anxious, or sad. But if you're feeling energetically prepared, what time of day should you be trying to read tarot? Or is it best to just go with your gut?

IN THE MORNINGS

Many tarot readers agree that the morning is the best time to read tarot. Generally, if you're planning on reading in the morning, you should read the cards right after you wake up or early on in your morning routine. This is because the idea behind reading the tarot cards in the morning is that you can apply them to the rest of your day, so you'll want to read them as early as possible.

Reading in the morning can be beneficial because your energy is completely fresh. When you read tarot cards as one of the first things you do during the day, you have unlimited energy resources to use on your cards. You also don't tend to have any negative emotions that could be affecting the cards you pull or your interpretation of them.

If you tend to notice that you're a morning person, wake up feeling fresh and reenergized, enjoy having a steady morning routine, or want to rely on tarot cards to help you address problems you face throughout the day, then pulling tarot cards in the morning might be the best time for you.

AT NIGHT

In the exact opposite of the morning tarot camp are the nighttime tarot readers. Many tarot readers enjoy pulling tarot cards as the very last thing they do during the day rather than the first. This is for a few reasons. First, nighttime tarot readers typically prefer to reflect on the events of the day and allow the tarot cards to help them process any issues they encountered earlier. They also use the cards to guide them through the decisions they'll make the following day. Plus, the energy they carry with them from the events of the day can affect the cards they pull, which will help them address the most pertinent issues of the day with the cards.

Another reason some people prefer to pull as the last thing they do during the day is so that they can consider the tarot cards while they sleep. Tarot cards are highly connected to energy levels, intuition, and the subconscious. Many readers like to pull at night so that they can ponder the cards while they sleep. They might try to analyze their dreams after a tarot reading or see if they wake up the next morning with any new thoughts. They may also simply allow their subconscious to analyze their tarot readings as they sleep, waking up having processed their emotions and the events of the day with the help of the cards.

AT A SPECIFIC TIME SIGNIFICANT TO YOU

If you have a time that is meaningful to you, an angel number you like to receive, or even a time of day where something meaningful happens, then this could be a good time to read tarot cards. For one, your energy levels will be more significant, and often more positive, if you focus on reading during a special time. This might even help to make your readings more unique.

Especially if you follow superstitions or if you have other spiritual beliefs, you may choose to tie these into your tarot card readings. There's nothing wrong with starting a reading at the time that represents your angel number or trying to perform a reading during your favorite time of day. These events can positively affect your energy levels and make you feel more prepared to interpret your reading.

AT EVENTFUL OR TRANSITIONAL ASTROLOGICAL TIMES

If you feel especially connected to astronomy or astrology, then you may choose to base your readings around the stars and planetary movements. Maybe you want to perform a reading as soon as the moon or sun rises or sets. Perhaps you choose to connect your reading to your zodiac sign—such as by reading under the light of the moon if you are a Cancer. You might perform your tarot reading around the same time as a significant astrological or astronomical event. Maybe you want to perform an extra powerful reading at the time of the full moon or during a lunar eclipse. All of these events can make you and your tarot readings more powerful.

THE DOS AND DON'TS OF GETTING A TAROT READING

Are you about to receive your first tarot reading? Are you new to the world of tarot and are wondering how to appropriately receive a tarot reading from someone else? Here are a few things you should and shouldn't do when you're the querent.

DO: RESEARCH YOUR READER

If you want to get a professional tarot reading, then you should research the person you're planning on getting a reading from beforehand. You'll first want to make sure you feel safe and comfortable enough with your tarot reader to give them your questions (especially if they're personal ones). You'll also want to make sure that their style of reading is what you're looking for. Do you want practical advice? A very open-ended interpretation? Are you a total beginner or do you want someone who won't completely guide you through the reading? These are all just a few questions you should consider when looking for a tarot reader.

DON'T: ASK UNANSWERABLE QUESTIONS

If you want your tarot reader to predict the future, tell you exactly what's going to happen when, or give you all the answers right away, you shouldn't be getting a tarot reading at all. The tarot reader can't fix your love life, your financials, or your career just by pulling a few cards. The idea behind tarot is that you can utilize what the cards tell you to make practical decisions.

See a card that's warning you of financial pitfalls? Maybe it's time to reexamine your savings accounts. Notice the cards are telling you there might be obstacles in your romantic life? You should try spending more time with your partner and having open, honest conversations with them. If you're approaching your tarot reader with questions like, "When will I get my promotion?" or "When and how will my partner propose?" you're in the wrong spot.

DO: FEEL FREE TO TELL YOUR READER WHAT YOU WANT ADVICE ON

If you're looking for something specific during your tarot session, you can let the reader know and see what they have to say. Though there are some questions that just can't be answered, that doesn't mean that you can't receive advice on a specific issue in your life. You might want advice pertaining to your finances or your professional career. Maybe you want to assess something that's been bothering you or get a peek into your subconscious mind. These are things the cards can help with, but it will help your tarot reader to know that this is what you want information on.

DON'T: ARGUE WITH THE READER

If you're not prepared to potentially pull negative tarot cards, then you shouldn't get a tarot reading. Negative cards don't always need to have a horrible, disastrous interpretation—but sometimes, you're going to pull them anyway. A good tarot reader may be able to find multiple interpretations for these cards that can better apply to your life. But you have to acknowledge and accept that sometimes, your reading might have things to say that aren't super positive. If you get this type of reading, there's no use in arguing with the tarot reader about it.

The same thing goes for the boundaries and rules the tarot reader sets. If they don't want to answer a certain question of yours or feel like they can't give you advice on a particular subject, it's not your place to argue with them. You can always find a different reader or just ask a different question.

DO: ACT ON YOUR READING

Tarot cards are meant to inspire change, not solidify your future. If you've received some negative tarot cards, it might be time to change your actions and reframe your thinking. This can help you change your current situation for the better.

Tarot cards will bring awareness to the things in your life you're struggling with. They might pull issues that only your subconscious can recognize or that you just haven't processed with. You might already know you have obstacles you need to deal with. Maybe you're just wondering what to prioritize first.

The tarot reader and their deck can help you leave understanding your reading and with a sense of direction on what to do next. Tarot cards cannot take away your free will; you can act in ways that will secure you a positive, happy future. So, even if you receive a reading that is on the negative side, take action: allow the cards to guide you towards growth and positive change.

HOW TO UNLOCK YOUR TRUE POTENTIAL USING THE MATRIX OF DESTINY

The Matrix of Destiny is a newer spiritual practice designed to give you all the information you could possibly need to actualize your goals, fulfill your life's purpose, and promote inner healing. Think of it as a spiritual personality test, if you will—a way to uncover your life's deeper meaning, discover your true path, and better understand your strengths and weaknesses.

The Matrix of Destiny is a complex visual designed to connect numerology, tarot cards, astrology, and chakras. All of these practices are deeply intertwined—from the way that zodiac signs' elements and tarot suits are intrinsically linked to how each Sun sign can be related to a different chakra.

By using your birthday (and sometimes your name when practicing certain strains of numerology), the Matrix of Destiny can reveal everything about your life's path, by taking all of your unique spiritual components—from your energetic alignments to your most relevant tarot cards—to give you significant information about yourself and your destiny.

The root numbers derived from your full birth date can be numerically linked to twenty-two different tarot cards in the Major Arcana—which includes cards like The Fool, The Empress, and The Wheel of Fortune. You'll also use your birthday to uncover more information about your astrological chart, and the numbers from your birthday (along with your zodiac sign) can tell you more about your chakras and energetic alignment.

Your Matrix of Destiny can help you understand specific areas of your life as they relate to your personality, your self-actualization goals, and your spiritual profile. It might give you insights about your potential regarding your financial future—where do you need to improve? What strengths lie in your future financial life path? How likely are you to be innately successful at making money based on your personal Matrix of Destiny alignment?

It might net you healing information about your relationships with others—from your romantic life to your familial bonds. If you've been wondering about how you process relationships, what your attachment type is, how your family ties impacted you growing up, and how to gain the most joy and peace from your romantic life, the Matrix of Destiny can tell you all about these things, too.

Because of the Matrix of Destiny's complex methodology, the Matrix is better suited to inform you of your true life's purpose. It categorizes your personal relationship with numerology, astrology, chakras, and tarot cards into different purposes and life guides—based on your personality, your attributes, and even your energetic alignments. Don't worry, it won't give you a specific career path or lay out all of your life's plans for you—but it will tell you the key areas you can focus on to feel satisfied with your life and self-fulfilled.

If you feel like you lack a purpose, are unsatisfied with where you are in life, or still have deep healing and processing work to do, the Matrix of Destiny might just be able to help you. It's the best way to receive a spiritual overview of your life as a whole—and it will even give you powerful actions and achievable goals to consider as you continue to age and grow

YOU NEED TO KNOW THESE 4 THINGS BEFORE READING TAROT CARDS ONLINE

If you're just getting into tarot readings or don't have access to a physical deck, you might be seeking online readings as an alternative. But before you decide to start practicing tarot online, there are a few things you need to consider.

YOUR ENERGY MAY NOT AFFECT THE CARDS

When practicing tarot, one important aspect of receiving a reading is allowing your energy to affect which cards you pull. A key part of this is physically touching the cards (or, if someone else is doing your reading for you, allowing their energy to interpret your questions on your behalf).

If you're 'pulling' cards from an online website, there is a lot of separation between you and the deck. Not only is the deck not physical, but there is also no way for you to energetically interact with it. This might change the readings you receive. It may also create barriers between you and the answers you seek; if you ask specific questions to an online tarot deck or are seeking advice in a specific area, you might be more likely to receive confusing or inaccurate answers.

To combat this, you might try to first ask less specific questions of your online tarot deck. You might also want to leave the readings much more open to interpretation and ensure you know all of the potential meanings of a card before trying to interpret it.

YOU MAY FEEL DISCONNECTED FROM THE DECK

A significant part of reading tarot is having a connection with your personal deck(s) of cards. They are yours to read from and likely have personal meaning to you. Whether you chose them because of their design or because they called to you specifically, practicing with the same deck over and over again can link you both energetically and spiritually.

When practicing with an online deck, this sense of ownership and practicing connection may be absent. You might not feel as strong of a tie to your tarot deck and may not feel the same spiritual connection when you do practice tarot. This could affect your readings, how often you practice, or just the significance you place on your tarot readings.

YOU MIGHT EXPERIENCE INTERRUPTIONS

One piece of the problem with many online tarot readings is that your reading might be affected by the site's layout. You might have your card pulling interrupted by advertisements, experience awkward site layouts, or have to wait a long time to draw a card. Especially when you're trying to connect meaningfully with the cards and interpret your reading without forced breaks, you might feel as though your connection with the cards has been severed if you're practicing tarot on a website that frequently disturbs your deck.

One way to work around this is to utilize a website—or even an app—that offers an advertisement-free experience or otherwise ensures that your tarot reading is uninterrupted as soon as you start actually pulling the cards. This can help ensure that your connection to the cards remains unsevered and that you can focus your energy entirely on the reading, immersing yourself in the deck.

YOU CAN'T PHYSICALLY ARRANGE THE CARDS

When you pull tarot cards, you may choose to do so in a specific spread. This layout can help you receive more information about a specific question or issue you've chosen to address. It can also help you ask multiple questions (especially ones related to each other) at once. The layout in which you pull the spread and then read those cards can change based on the questions you're asking and the energy you're reading cards with. You may have a favorite spread or vary the spread you pull each day.

However, online websites usually do not offer an opportunity for you to choose the spread you pull. Most online tarot websites will pull one card from a virtual 'deck' for you at a time before either stacking or reshuffling the deck and allowing you to draw again. This means that you don't get to choose a spread that speaks to you and that you won't have the opportunity to ask specific questions that relate to a tarot spread. For some, this may not be a big deal. But for others, lacking the ability to try a tarot spread can mean a large part of the tarot experience is missing.

If you are planning on getting more into tarot, it might be a good idea to purchase or borrow a physical deck yourself. If you have no access to one, note that playing cards can also be used as tarot cards! You may also choose to opt for online readings with a real person instead of a website. Do your research on the person you pick to perform a reading for you, but know that many people may offer free readings online—especially in exchange for streaming or recording your reading for others to participate in

WHAT TO DO WHEN YOU DON'T UNDERSTAND YOUR TAROT CARD READING

CONSULT THE CARDS

If you've pulled an answer you don't understand, you can always ask the deck for more clarity on the advice you've received. Don't be afraid to ask clarifying questions or just continue pulling additional cards until you get a better sense of how the first card(s) you pulled was meant to be interpreted.

You can start by pulling just one additional descriptor card or pull several (many querents like to pull in groups of three or other small numbers that are significant to them) until you feel satisfied in understanding the meaning of your original tarot card. That doesn't mean you're going to be pulling new cards for hours and hours on end—you should receive more clarity within another card or three.

ASK A FRIEND

When we try to read our own tarot cards, it can be difficult. There may be things about our current situations that our brains just don't want to recognize—there could be something subconscious that we're not ready to address yet or we might just be missing an obvious piece of the puzzle because we're too close to the issue to see it for what it is.

Consulting a friend for advice can help you find additional meanings and interpretations of your reading that you might not have thought of before. You can even ask tarot groups online or on social media for their opinion of your pull, although you may receive varying levels of advice.

GO FOR ANOTHER READING

If you can't understand the cards you've pulled yourself, you may want to opt to have someone else perform your reading. One issue with reading cards yourself is that, if you read in times of stress or emotional turmoil, you may be confusing the energy of the cards as you pull them. This can result in muddled or unclear readings. Your emotional state can even make it difficult to interpret the cards you've drawn (even if they feel right for you).

Receiving another reading from someone else might help you reassure yourself with a new understanding of what the cards mean. This way, you can both consult the tarot reader for advice on what your original reading might have meant and see what new cards pop up. If you pull the same cards during your second reading, you'll at least have someone else there to help you interpret them more clearly.

TRY AGAIN

There's nothing wrong with scrapping an unclear reading and trying again. You may pull one or two of the same cards during your second reading, but ideally, you'll pull either an entirely new set or you'll pull new cards alongside your original card(s) that can help you clarify what the deck is trying to tell you.

If you pulled just a few tarot cards during your first reading, you may decide to pull more during your second to help you understand the deck better. On the other hand, if pulling too many cards during your first reading confused their meaning, you might decide to pull just one to three cards this time so you can focus on what they're really trying to say.

THINK ON IT

When you come across a card you just can't understand in your current situation, you may want to tuck it away in the back of your mind for later. When you're presented with a new obstacle, challenge, or situation you want advice on, think back to the card you couldn't understand earlier. Does it have a new meaning? Is there a way it can be applied to your current situation?

You don't need to think about your tarot card reading forever—and of course, you can always perform a new reading if there are new situations you want to seek advice on. But there may be a time where a reading you didn't quite understand at first becomes perfectly clear later on. Even sleeping for a night or two on the meaning of your tarot pull might help you unravel some of its purpose.

A POSITIVE SPIN ON SOME OF THE WORST TAROT CARDS TO RECEIVE

DEATH

When you receive this card upright, you might think that it signifies illness or fear the worst when it comes to you and your loved ones. But fear not—the death card is not here to signify literal death, and it does have a very positive interpretation.

The Death card typically signifies change. Death means the metaphorical death of the things that no longer serve you; it means letting go, accepting change, and, later, seeing the results of your growth. By the Death card's standard, it can be a massively beneficial card to receive; it might even be guiding you towards changes you already want to make and helping you set free things you are already ready to let go of.

THREE OF SWORDS

The Three of Swords is an unwelcome card for many. It typically signifies immense grief, heartbreak, and loss of an important relationship. For those looking for romantic advice or those going through tough times, the Three of Swords is a card you probably don't want to see.

But tarot cards aren't here to predict the future; they're here to help you overcome your current situation. Remember that the Swords suit represents your intellect and your heart. The Three of Swords might be warning you about your own emotions—for example, they could tell you that your anxiety is impacting your relationship, that you should rely on yourself in times of trouble, or that processing through grieving is okay. The Three of Swords is a reminder that bad things can always happen, but that we keep moving forward regardless.

FIVE OF CUPS

The Five of Cups is a card of grief. It's known to represent both sadness and loss. Some readers also note the Five of Cups as a symbol of the querent having regrets.

You can, however, look at the Five of Cups positively. For one, the Five of Cups serves to draw your attention both towards the things you spend too much time regretting and those that you should be more thankful for. The Five of Cups may look bleak at first glance, but it does bring advice with it to find abundance and gratefulness in what you do have with you still.

The Five of Cups is not just about allowing grief but about finding the positive regardless of your struggles. In times of regret, the Five of Cups reminds you to recall things you can appreciate without allowing your regret to cloud your vision.

HERE ARE THE BEST TIMES TO PULL TAROT CARDS

If you're new to tarot cards or are just looking to get some new insights, one question on your mind might be whether or not there's a certain time you should be reading tarot cards. Many tarot readers agree that pulling cards at a certain time of day can help them focus more, gain more understanding, and even have more clarity about what their reading might mean. Here are a few ideas you can follow if you're thinking about pulling your tarot at a specific time.

IN THE EVENING

Evenings are a popular time to pull tarot. Not only will pulling tarot at night give you the opportunity to reflect on your day, it can also provide you with more clarity on the day's events and prepare you for what's ahead. You might have new things on your mind that you want to settle before going to sleep—pulling tarot in the evening can also give you time to sort out your thoughts around what the cards you pull might mean.

Some tarot readers swear by pulling cards just before they go to sleep, allowing them to think about the cards as they sleep and wake up with new solutions. Allowing your subconscious to take over the interpretation can give you clarity you might not have found otherwise.

IN THE MORNING

In the opposite camp are the tarot readers who want to begin their day with a fresh reading. Many querents want to approach the day ahead with cards in mind. Even if they don't wake up with a specific question they want to have answered, some readers believe that the cards they pull in the morning should be kept in mind throughout the day, giving them potential solutions to utilize later.

Morning tarot readers may also prefer to pull early on so that they can allow the tarot cards to influence their day as needed. If you're pulling tarot cards that focus on specific aspects of your life—love, career, finances—then you may want to dedicate more time, energy, or focus to that area of your life. Pulling tarot cards in the morning could allow you to plan your day in a way that allows you to pay attention to something you've been neglecting.

WHEN YOUR INTUITION TELLS YOU TO

If you're not in a particular camp of wanting to pull tarot in the morning or at night, you might be wondering when, exactly, you should look to the cards. Many readers choose a daily routine of pulling either in the morning or night in order to establish a rhythm, but there's nothing wrong with pulling only as needed.

Especially if you're not planning on reading tarot cards every day or if you're in a situation where you frequently look to the cards for guidance, you may want to wait until you have something specific to resolve to seek out advice from your card deck. This means that you would intentionally avoid scheduling a certain time for you to pull cards, and instead wait for a situation to pop up where you feel you could use their guidance.

Acting intuitively will give you more control over the questions you ask the cards and the type of advice you seek from them. There's also nothing wrong with choosing a specific time of day (or two!) to pull cards regularly while still reading them whenever your intuition tells you to.

PERSONALITY

Your guide to every sign under the sun.

3 ZODIAC SIGNS WHO STRUGGLE WITH CONFIDENCE (BUT SHOULDN'T)

VIRGO

Virgo, your constant strive for the unattainable can sometimes undermine your confidence. It may be natural for you to notice every minor flaw or oversight, but remember, the rest of the world rarely sees things as critically as you do. You're a remarkably high achiever, but it's so easy for you to recognize the little details that you might end up feeling like your work isn't worth anything if it's not completely perfect. Just keep in mind that nobody else sees it that way, Virgo—even those who are scrutinizing your accomplishments probably still won't find any mistakes!

CANCER

Cancer, you're great at connecting deeply with others, but this same desire to listen to other people can also make you susceptible to external opinions. Sometimes, you might find yourself doubting your decisions or worth based on perceived judgments or casual remarks from others. The emotional depth you possess is a double-edged sword—it allows you to love deeply and understand others, but it also can make you vulnerable to thoughts that aren't even your own. You'll have to learn to trust your own opinion, Cancer; you're allowed to seek insights and support from those who care for you, but at the end of the day, your life is your own. It'll take work, but you'll get there.

PISCES

Pisces, your fluid nature can sometimes make you feel uncertain about your place in the world. While your creativity is unparalleled, it can sometimes leave you feeling unanchored, leading to bouts of self-doubt and questions about your purpose and path. You might feel like you have a lot of dreams that are totally unachievable, or like your life is better lived in your head rather than in reality. You might find it helpful to learn how to ground yourself in times like these—walking the line between your own desires and reality can be a delicate balancing act, so it's not your fault if you feel uncertain about where you lie sometimes. Take the time to appreciate your life for what it is—dreams and all—and take baby steps toward making your real world just as appealing as your dreams.

3 ZODIAC SIGNS WHO CAN BE INTIMIDATING TO INTERACT WITH

SCORPIO

Scorpio, you can be difficult to engage in conversation due to your naturally intense and secretive nature. You're not always forthcoming with your feelings and prefer to keep your cards close to your chest. Your skepticism can also make you wary of small talk or superficial conversations, often leading you to shut down or retreat into your shell. To make yourself more approachable, you should keep in mind that not all conversations require depth or introspection. Sometimes, surface-level interactions are necessary to build rapport and establish trust. By learning to be more open and less suspicious, you can create more fulfilling connections and open up a pathway to the deeper interactions you crave.

CAPRICORN

You can sometimes be challenging to communicate with due to your pragmatic—and occasionally aloof—demeanor. You tend to be goal-oriented and focused on practical matters, which can make your conversation style come off as rigid or impersonal. Your high standards and critical nature can also be intimidating, making others hesitant to engage with you (even though you mean well!).

For you to become more approachable, Capricorn, you should strive to incorporate more flexibility and empathy into your communication style. Understanding that not all conversations have to be productive can help you connect more authentically with others. Also, showing a bit more vulnerability will make others feel more comfortable around you.

AQUARIUS

Aquarius, with your unique and independent mindset, you can be a little tough to converse with. You often have unconventional views and a futuristic perspective that can be hard for others to understand. Your desire for intellectual stimulation can make small talk or common topics seem mundane to you, causing you to disengage or come across as distant and indifferent.

To be more approachable, you should keep in mind that not every conversation has to revolve around intellectual discussions! Embracing the simplicity of everyday conversations and showing genuine interest in others' perspectives will help you establish more meaningful connections. Also, tempering your tendency to detach or disconnect when the conversation isn't stimulating enough will make you more accessible and inviting to others.

4 ZODIAC SIGNS THAT EVERYONE UNDERESTIMATES (BUT SHOULDN'T)

CANCER

When it comes to your professional abilities, Cancer, you can sometimes fly under the radar, overshadowed by more assertive signs like Aries or Capricorn. Your empathetic personality makes you seem more suited for roles that involve caregiving or support. But don't be fooled, Cancer—you possess an incredible intuition, allowing you to excel in fields that require keen insight and decision-making. Your dedication to your work, coupled with your tenacity, makes you a formidable opponent in any setting, especially when you're driven by passion.

VIRGO

Virgo, you're often typecast as the meticulous, detail-oriented sign, sometimes even reduced to the role of 'the nitpicker'. While your analytical nature is well-documented, what's frequently overlooked is your ability to see the bigger picture. In corporate settings, you might be overshadowed by signs like Taurus or Libra, who come across as more dominant leaders. Yet, it's often the Virgo in the room who strategizes and streamlines processes with precision. Your methodical thought process, combined with your knack for communication, also makes you a highly effective educator, speaker, and writer.

CAPRICORN

Capricorn, you're universally acknowledged for your work ethic. However, you're often pigeonholed into roles that demand discipline and rigor, while your versatility is underestimated. In fields dominated by charismatic signs like Sagittarius or Leo, Capricorns might seem less glamorous. Yet, your grounded nature allows you to excel in roles that require both creativity and structure, like architectural design or film direction. In interpersonal relationships, your reserved nature can sometimes be mistaken for aloofness or a lack of passion. This couldn't be further from the truth—your stoicism might overshadow your warmth, but your dedicated love for your work and relationships perseveres.

LIBRA

Libra, with your inherent charm, you're often deemed as a people-pleaser or diplomatic to a fault. You're sometimes underestimated in competitive fields, with more aggressive signs like Scorpio or Aries seemingly holding the upper hand. However, your ability to mediate and see multiple sides of an issue can make them top-tier negotiators, ideal for roles in international diplomacy or corporate mergers. Your natural sense of balance and ability to navigate any tense situation with grace is often so well-executed it's barely noticeable; this can cause others to underestimate your abilities (sometimes in a way that leaves you with the upper hand). Your skills are a blend of intellect and artistry that shouldn't be underestimated.

THESE ZODIAC SIGNS DON'T RESPOND WELL TO CHANGE—BUT THEY CAN LEARN TO

VIRGO

As someone who enjoys meticulously planning their day, change isn't always a good thing to you, Virgo. You can often prepare for larger changes in your life when you can control them, which allows you to accept and appreciate them more. But when things happen spontaneously or are out of your control, you often struggle to accept that you can't really do much about it.

The great thing is that you can learn to adapt to change—you're a sign who isn't entirely inflexible, and you're great at preparing for new plans on the fly. Another bonus is that you usually come prepared for anything, which can help you preemptively adapt to small changes that happen spontaneously. The best way for you to learn to accept and appreciate change is by letting go of some control of the situation. Learning to prepare for what you can and accepting that anything else is out of your hands might take some weight off your shoulders—you can memorize a tow truck number, but you can't stop the car from breaking down.

TAURUS

Your zodiac sign is basically the hallmark of being change-avoidant. You like your schedule, your cozy space, your routines, your comfort hobbies. You tend to be more introverted and enjoy quieter activities—like cooking or gardening. Changes big and small can sometimes terrify you because so many things are outside of your comfort zone.

That doesn't mean you can't find success and comfort within change, though. Change is often easiest for you when you can focus on changing one thing at a time, so that you'll still have many of the same creature comforts to rely on. It's easy to say that you should push yourself out of your comfort zone to help you adapt to changes more easily, but that can be daunting for many—not just you, Taurus! If you're struggling to get out of your comfort zone but still have to deal with change, the best thing to do is give yourself the time and space to accept the changes that are happening—even if they're positive changes. Rely on your typical creature comforts as much as possible during turbulent periods, and take comfort in slow, deliberate days and activities that bring you as much peace as possible.

CANCER

As a Cancer, you're a sensitive and sentimental sign. You don't always respond negatively to change—especially when it comes to positive changes or periods of growth—but you can still have a hard time with it every once in a while. For you, the main culprit is nostalgia. You want to reminisce about old memories all the time, which can make the changes that happen in your life harder to manage. You feel things deeply, which can make it seem as though small changes are enormous and have completely turned over your life. Your sentimentality often has you living in the past for short periods.

Contrary to what you may think, nostalgia and sentimentality are healthy emotions when taken in short doses. Someone has to be the photo-taker and the album-keeper of your social circle, after all! Change feels different for everyone, and it might actually be comforting for you to reminisce on old times. Just make sure that you're living in and for the present, not the past—take the time to be sentimental when the mood strikes, but don't allow it to overwhelm you. Focus on the positive things about your current life that you never thought you'd accomplish in the past moments you're reminiscing on—you'll see how much you've grown over the changes that have happened in your life.

THESE ZODIAC SIGNS ARE NO-NONSENSE TYPES

CAPRICORN

You're often perceived as stoic and unemotional because of your dedication to your work and your ambition. You tend to be a highly serious type—especially when you're focused. Even in your personal life, you're no-nonsense about the things you love; you dedicate time to your hobbies and are loyal to your loved ones. You don't have time for messing around and rarely take anything for granted. This makes you a highly unique zodiac sign, one who tends to have a well-organized and appreciated life. In your case, being no-nonsense isn't necessarily a bad thing.

SCORPIO

It's fair to say that you're not always a no-nonsense kind of person. But when you're truly focused on something or dedicated to a particular cause, you become serious in a way that no other sign can mimic. Whether you're taking charge of a social situation or going for a promotion at work, it's almost scary how quickly you can shift from being a little looser to becoming very intense about your life. As long as you know when to relax a little bit, though, this mindset shift can actually help you lock into your goals and achieve your dreams.

AQUARIUS

You can definitely be quirky and goofy at times, Aquarius. But when it comes to your general personality—especially when you're working—you tend to be no-nonsense and highly logical. You rarely act from your emotions and focus primarily on the logic of a situation, even when it comes to your own personal comfort. This can make you ruthless when it comes to your ambitions, because you know exactly what you need to do to realistically get what you want. But this can make you a little intense to work with, especially when it comes to your loved ones being affected by stressful times at work.

TAURUS

Despite loving cozy things, aesthetic things, and whatever else makes you comfortable, you can also be surprisingly no-nonsense. You're the sign of the bull, after all. This makes you just as stubborn as you are reliable and grounded. When you're ready to seize a goal, win an argument, or have found something you want, others around you might agree that you undergo a sudden change. Though you can sometimes be defensive and quick to anger, you also become intensely serious and no-nonsense during these kinds of situations. Additionally, because you're a grounded and responsible sign, you can usually be relied upon in stressful scenarios, making you a level-headed kind of person who won't tolerate nonsense.

THESE 3 ZODIAC SIGNS FEAR BEING ALONE

CANCER

As an intuitive water sign, you rely on your friends and family for support and emotional connection. One of your main love languages is acts of service—caring and supporting others you feel close to is extremely important to you. You wouldn't feel the same without your friend group's traditions or family holidays. Having a romantic partner is also often a high priority for your sign. This also means that—as a sign that can sometimes be a worrier—one of your greatest fears is being left alone. Whether you're scared you'll never find true love or just always feel like your friend group secretly doesn't want you around, you often give into your own anxieties around being left behind.

SCORPIO

At first glance, you might seem like a slightly solitary sign. Your sign can range from introverted to extroverted. You're extremely charming socially, so you may have plenty of friends or just be popular at parties, but you also struggle to open up to people. You may feel that you have fewer genuine connections than most people or that it takes you too long to open up to those around you. This can exacerbate your fear of being alone—for you, Scorpio, you can still feel lonely even in a crowd of people. You need people you can genuinely connect with in order to avoid feeling alone—and when it's hard for you to open up to people, it can worsen the fear that you'll end up with no one.

PISCES

Your imagination and intuition often changes with your mood. You're an empathetic person that needs other people around you to feel supported in life. Your creativity, mood, and even your dreams can change based on how socially supported you feel. As someone who is so intuitive that you even lean towards overthinking things, you might often find yourself feeling anxious over the thought of being left alone. You're also a hopeless romantic, which often makes you worry over finding the right partner for yourself. Your imagination can sometimes even cause you to think of negative thoughts and outcomes around social situations, which creates an even bigger fear of being left alone.

IF YOUR ZODIAC SIGN IS ON THIS LIST, YOU'RE ALWAYS THE LISTENER

CANCER

You often take it upon yourself to nurture other people by listening to their feelings. You feel it's your duty, even if other people don't specifically ask you to do so. As someone who is naturally shy—and can sometimes even come across as reserved in group settings—you may feel most comfortable when you're listening to someone else as opposed to sharing. You like having a goal in a conversation that doesn't mean you have to speak about yourself—you might take it upon yourself to let someone else vent, try to placate them, resolve an argument, or make them feel better about something.

This is an honorable task that your friends and family no doubt appreciate, but they might not realize that in the process, they're losing out on knowing about you, too. A difficult thing for many listeners to understand is that those who are not listeners don't understand that sometimes, you feel an inability to speak—not just a dislike of speaking up. It can be hard for you to want to compete for a spot in the conversation. One-on-one discussions are where you flourish most, and this can be a good way to connect more deeply with those you care about.

LIBRA

In group contexts, you're always the listener. You might find that opposing sides of an argument will always seek you out to settle tensions. Like you're the parent of the group, you find yourself having to listen to all sides of an argument and come up with a solution on the fly to keep everyone happy. As the reigning ruler of compromises, most of your time is spent listening, not actually talking.

You take it upon yourself to relieve everyone else of the burdens of their problems. It admittedly does feel pretty good for your sign to resolve a conflict, but when that doesn't happen, you're usually the one who shoulders the most weight of the argument. Even when peaceful resolutions do happen, devoting your energy to so much listening can be exhausting—especially when you weren't even involved in the original conflict! If you really want to help, you can always opt to give a few pointers and resources to those that come to you for advice before washing your hands of the situation. But you certainly wouldn't be in the wrong to take a break from your role as impromptu advisor for a while.

VIRGO

Most of your time is spent offering advice to others, Virgo. As a practical sign with a solution for everything, it's natural for others to want to seek you out when they have a problem. The issue is, everyone who's seeking a one-on-one session with you can't see how many other people you're trying to deal with, too. You might feel more like a confessional than a friend on some days, especially when you devote yourself to fixing multiple big problems for different people all at once.

That's not to say that you shouldn't share your pragmatism with those you care about, but you don't need to force yourself to be a sounding board for other people, either. It can be useful for others to vent to you or talk out their problems, but you should be getting the same level of reciprocation from them. One problem Virgos often run into is that they feel like they can solve all of their own problems, so they don't need to talk about it with anyone else. In that case, you should preserve your energy when trying to solve others' issues for them—and make sure that you're still seeing conversational reciprocation, too.

TAURUS

An introverted, peaceful sign, you're often the person others turn to for a bit of solace and advice. You live a calming, cozy life—your sign is often known for being a good gardener and a good cook, both of which might make people find you more approachable. You don't mind talking about yourself, but often find yourself being talked over instead. Whether or not you'll speak up for yourself truly depends—as the sign of the bull, you can become stubborn on issues you care about, but the chances of everyone you speak to seeing that spark are slim.

To protect that peace you cherish so much in your daily life, you'll need to limit the conversations you can have with others about their own issues. You're a great person to vent to, Taurus—you know all the right places to agree and validate others' feelings—but that doesn't mean you have to listen like it's a full-time job. You'll need to look for people who can not only respect your boundaries, but also respect your conversation style. If you want reciprocation from your social circle by being given the space to rant about your hobbies or discuss your career, you deserve that too.

IF YOU'RE ONE OF THESE ZODIAC SIGNS, YOU NEED TO BE MORE PATIENT

SAGITTARIUS

With your love of adventure and spontaneity, you rarely have any patience. Whether you're waiting for the work day to end or getting ready to start your next adventure, you just can't wait to jump right into the next thing on your schedule. You might even be guilty of planning your next vacation while you're still on one. Your sign always needs to have something fun to look forward to, which can make you feel impatient no matter what you're doing. But since you're always looking ahead, try to appreciate the fact that you have so many new things to look forward to. Your sign will always be partaking in a new experience soon enough, and sometimes the wait to do something special makes it even more worthwhile.

GEMINI

You have to keep yourself busy to stay entertained, Gemini. When you stick with something for too long, it loses its shine—you always want a new passion, hobby, interest, and professional project to keep your mind active. This makes you highly impatient—when you're done with something, you're totally done. You want to move on right away, and hate having to stick with things for longer than your mind wants to. You often lose motivation too, which only makes you less patient. Though this generally gives you an interesting personal and social life, it can cause problems when it comes to your career. The best thing you can do for yourself is to keep your interests varied and unique outside of work so that you can focus on long-term professional projects when you need to.

ARIES

Your competitive nature and spontaneous personality both mean that patience is not always your best friend, Aries. Though you're highly dedicated toward your goals and usually don't mind pursuing one thing for a long time if it means success, you can still struggle with being patient at times. You always want to achieve the next biggest or best thing, and you're always chasing new successes. You don't wait to celebrate one achievement before immediately planning another one, and the time between making goals and achieving them seems to stretch far too long for your liking. You're always on the move and have endless energy, so any time spent not doing a million things at once (successfully, to boot) feels like time wasted. But you should get used to relaxing every once in a while and celebrating your achievements when you can. This can help you understand how far you've already come, re-motivating you towards your current goals and helping you be a little more patient with yourself at times.

YOUR MENTAL AGE, BASED ON YOUR ZODIAC SIGN

ARIES

You have the drive and passion of a young self-starter that everyone can see success in, yet the leadership skills and power of someone with many professional years under your belt. Combining these two things puts you in your thirties, with a level head and good sense of self, but still with much spontaneity, excitement, and competition to spice up your life. You'll see these benefits both in your professional life and when it comes to your personal passions, too.

TAURUS

You might just be an old soul at heart, Taurus. With your love of cozy, quiet hobbies, your tendency to lean toward things like cooking and crafting, and your deep sense of loyalty and responsibility, your mental age places you in your sixties. You still experience bursts of sudden stubbornness when it comes to your passions (or anything that really grinds your gears), but you're also a deeply peaceful sign that enjoys living a loving, genuine life.

GEMINI

It's your sense of curiosity and almost childlike wonder that gives your sign a young mental age, Gemini. This is a good thing for you—it keeps you learning (and might explain why you bounce around from interest to interest). You're highly connected to your inner child, yet still retain a sense of maturity that keeps you driven in your daily life, lending energy to your dual nature.

Practically, your mental age can vary, but when it comes to your curiosity and exploration, there's no doubt that your mental age is even younger than a preteen.

CANCER

You tend to be in your forties or fifties when it comes to your mental age, Cancer. You're still a deeply sensitive soul, and may carry with you many wounds from your childhood years. But your caring nature and your tendency to want to nurture those you're close to make you mentally a little older. You place immense value on your friends and family and do your best to carefully foster and grow each of these relationships with the sincerity and effort that someone with life experience will. But you still tend to be emotional and can often be overwhelmed by your own empathy at times, which can vary your mental age slightly within the middle aged range.

LEO

With your flair for drama and your interest in being the center of attention, you tend to carry a more childlike mental age, Leo. You're a creative person who has a unique and joyous sense of self-expression, preferring to set your own trends rather than follow others' lead. This gives you the best of the best when it comes to your childlike tendencies, as it gives you your bold sense of identity and natural confidence that simply never grows old. Your mental age can easily stretch from preteen to teenager.

VIRGO

It's probably not much of a surprise to you that your sign tends to be mentally older. With your knack for organization and your love of methodology, you just can't help but be the responsible one. This makes you intelligent beyond your years, whether you're the parent of your friend group or just seem to have every skill you need for the perfect home and professional life. Generally, you tend to sit around the mid-fifties when it comes to your mental age, Virgo.

LIBRA

Your social skills, grace, and maturity pin you right around the age of thirty, Libra. You're skilled and often a successful professional, yet you still struggle with setting boundaries and understanding how to advocate for yourself. Your mental age is that of an adult who's still learning about themselves; you tend to be more responsible and carry a deep sense of your own values with you, but you don't always know how to defend yourself.

SCORPIO

Your sign often has a mental age of late thirties to early forties, although this mental age can vary depending on your sign's personal interests and habits. Your deep connection with your inner self and the time it takes you to trust others makes you a more cautious—and even wiser—sign. But your sign also has tendencies towards being jealous, manipulative, and seeking control over social situations. These facets of your personality place you at a very young age, typically in your teens. When you skew more towards seeking a quiet, authentic understanding of life and those around you, your sign's mental age is middle-aged. But if you notice you're a Scorpio that possesses more of those other qualities, you're likely to be much, much mentally younger than most signs.

SAGITTARIUS

Your sign can be a bit of a toss-up, Sagittarius. The reason for this is because you have childlike tendencies toward spontaneity and exploration, but you also have a profound sense of wisdom and love of philosophy that makes you wiser than most other signs. You carry with you a very youthful, optimistic way of looking at the world that keeps you young at heart no matter what, yet you also seem to have wisdom that stretches far beyond your own age. Your wise side could put you in your fifties or sixties, while your spontaneity keeps you forever in your twenties.

CAPRICORN

Your mental age tends to pin you right around forty, Capricorn. You have a good head on your shoulders, a strong ambition, and probably have many accomplishments already behind you. At the same time, you still tend to overthink things and allow your anxiety to dictate your preparations when it comes to much of your life. You're not at the point of not caring about what others think of you or overcoming all of your worries, but you're certainly an impressively disciplined and accomplished person, giving you a middle-aged mentality.

AQUARIUS

Your complex personality puts you in your mid-thirties, Aquarius. You're someone who tends to be young at heart, though you also have a logical and stoic side to you that might make someone think your mental age is in your fifties or sixties at first glance. But your drive to embrace the future and be a forward-thinker, your tendency to cast aside tradition, and your ever-evolving sense of self keeps you forever young. This makes mid-thirties the right mental age for you, Aquarius.

PISCES

Your mental age tends to place you in your early twenties. You're a dreamer, Pisces, there's no doubt about that. You have big dreams and are ready to defy reality in order to achieve them. Your creative energy and wild imagination places you right at the age of someone who can still embrace the wonder of their childhood yet has the power and potential to achieve every dream they have. It's a beautiful place full of possibilities for you to land, Pisces.

THESE 4 ZODIAC SIGNS AREN'T BIG PARTIERS

CANCER

Cancer tends to be more towards the introverted side of the zodiac, and they're generally the type to prefer a quiet night in. They're sensitive, highly empathetic, and often feel responsible for everyone else in the group. This means that Cancer is most likely to be doing the planning, being the designated driver, and spending their entire night keeping track of everyone to make sure things are going well. This makes their nights out more about personal responsibility than having fun. Also, Cancer can often get overwhelmed easily, which makes crowded clubs less entertaining for them than a nice night in.

CAPRICORN

Capricorn can be emotionally stoic. They're not big on long nights out on the town—their idea of 'letting loose' is relaxing in a quieter environment to take some time to recharge. Generally, with Capricorn's focus on work and personal goals, their time off is spent doing something they feel helps them rest and prevents them from becoming burnt out. For most Capricorns, this means intentional time with loved ones—at home, over dinner, or at a more calming activity than a party.

VIRGO

Virgo can be a highly introverted sign. They tend to spend their down time organizing their mind, on productive hobbies, or enjoying some DIY projects. To them, having a healthy routine is important—they'd rather do some journaling and go to bed early than hit the town. This zodiac sign is probably busy having early dinners and getting ready to wake up at the crack of dawn for a productive day. Though they're good communicators, Virgo doesn't always love socializing in large groups. Also, when they need to recharge their energy, they tend to prefer being alone for a while, or else they feel like they can't catch a break.

SCORPIO

Though this sign can be both social and charming, they don't always tend to enjoy parties. They're good at commanding social situations and are often best around their friends, but this doesn't mean they like large groups where they don't know anyone. This sign can range from highly introverted to extroverted, but they still tend to prefer one-on-one connections that are more genuine. This makes them less attracted to party scenarios and more interested in finding activities that allow them personal bonding time with their friends. Even if they're looking to meet new people, they generally won't want to do so at a party. They'd rather spend their night relaxing inside, saving the socializing for later.

THESE ARE THE 'JACK OF ALL TRADES' ZODIAC SIGNS

GEMINI

Of course you're first on this list, Gemini. Your activities are as diverse as your schedule is busy, and you prefer things that way. Your sign is known for being curious, which leads you to want to try something new all the time. Plus, as the sign of the twin, you often have changing and wildly varied interests—almost like two personalities are fighting over which hobbies you should pick. Your sign also tends to be so interested in trying new things that you don't end up sticking with older projects for very long, leaving you to be the jack of all trades but master of none. Don't forget how this quote really ends, though—oftentimes better than a master of one!

SAGITTARIUS

Because you're always craving a new adventure, you often don't end up sticking with something for long. This leaves you with an ever-changing roster of cool skills and experiences. Maybe you picked up a niche sport for a few months, followed along with the strangest hobby you could find in your area, or went on a long adventure to a few countries you'd never been to before. Over time, as these things become more familiar to you, your brain starts to lose interest. At the same time, it also finds other, newer activities to be more intriguing. You're probably used to the cycle of finding something that interests you, learning the ropes, improving, and then dropping it for something else. This leaves you with a lot of unique skills without much mastery in one particular area.

AQUARIUS

Okay, Aquarius, you might be a master of one thing—but you're also rotating through a vast landscape of projects, interests, and hobbies. You're generally able to stick with one singular interest for a long time, be it a professional career or a personal project, but your other passions rotate out at a rapid-fire pace. Because your interests gear towards academic ones (and you tend to connect with others the most over shared hobbies and interests), you end up bouncing around across a variety of projects, books, and skill sets. Maybe you picked up beginner coding or started learning about philosophy, but quickly got sucked into a volunteering project that ended so you could learn video editing. Your quirks lead you to pick out unique and uncommon hobbies that you want to learn more about—sometimes you stay long enough to perfect them, but as long as the itch to learn more is satisfied, you're usually ready to move on after just a little while.

THESE ZODIAC SIGNS NEVER KNOW WHAT THEY WANT

GEMINI

The sign of the twin is often known for being conflicted and indecisive. You've got a lot on your to-do list and always jump around from one activity to another. You can't seem to stay still, but you also can't seem to figure out what they want. You sometimes end up trying to do everything at once, while other times you spend too long deciding and don't end up doing anything at all. Though you have endless amounts of interests, passions, and curiosities, you never really seem to know what you want from most of them.

SAGITTARIUS

Your sign often has a tough time deciding on things because you're spontaneous and love freedom. When something threatens your schedule, you tend to pass it by. This makes you indecisive about your career and even about certain hobbies. You like to leave things open to opportunity—which ironically means you miss out on committed activities.

LIBRA

Your sign is known for being indecisive. You usually take others' opinions into account too frequently when you're trying to make a decision. When it comes to your morals and personal values, you often have an easy time figuring out what is right (and what action you want to take). But if other people are involved, you struggle to speak up for yourself. It can also seem confusing for you because you may genuinely not be able to decipher whether you're choosing an option because you want it or because the other people in your group do.

THESE ZODIAC SIGNS CAN NEVER FINISH A BOOK

GEMINI

You're probably a major bookworm yourself, Gemini. You're always finding a new hobby or topic that interests you, and, true to your sign, you want to learn more about it right away. The only problem is that your constant curiosity is always pushing you towards new subjects, not forcing you to finish what you've started on old ones. You might furiously dedicate yourself towards one new subject in a particular week and then randomly drop it for something completely different on a whim. That's definitely not a bad thing, but it does make summing up your Goodreads each year a bit challenging—do you think you can count two half-read books as one?

SAGITTARIUS

Your sign is very wise, loves to read, and is even likely to be interested in philosophy. You actually do have long periods where you can get lucky and finish everything that you've started, but, as a sign who's always looking for a new adventure, you often struggle to finish what you're reading. Sometimes you lose interest partway through and sometimes you accidentally put a book down only to never get around to finishing it again. You also often leave books for so long that you can't remember what they were about by the time you get back around to them again. It's just a result of your spontaneity.

AQUARIUS

With a quirky personality and set interests, it might seem a little surprising for others to hear that you sometimes can't finish reading a book that you've put down. But you tend to be very focused on your work and physical passions, which means that reading sometimes falls to the very end of your to-do list. You also tend to pick longer and more complex works, which means that you have to dedicate more time out of your day to read them. Additionally, you might be the kind of sign who picks a book based off of a specific piece of information you want to learn from it—and once you've hit that chapter, you're done reading. You're known to be a quirky sign, so you likely have a hefty collection of intriguing titles, but that doesn't mean you've made your way through them all just yet.

YES, THESE ZODIAC SIGNS WILL ALWAYS CRY AT MOVIES

CANCER

Cancer is a sensitive sign, and they're highly empathetic towards others—even if those other people are actors on a film screen. They're always going to cry at sad commercials, sad movies, and possibly even happy movies, too. If you're sat next to them on the couch or at the theater, expect to be passing tissues regularly. The movies that will probably make them cry most usually involve animals, tragic romance stories, or movies that focus on family themes.

PISCES

As an empathetic type, Pisces is rarely one to hold back your emotions during a movie. This makes the experience more exciting for them—they feel genuine fear during a horror movie, pain at tragic endings, and happiness when they see a fairytale romance on screen. It's usually the sad stuff that will make Pisces cry. Profound and moving stories will always be tearjerkers for them, although their sign might find themselves tearing up at less devastating storylines, too.

SCORPIO

Believe it or not, Scorpio can actually be a big crier during movies—they just might not show it. If they're around large groups, especially of people they don't know that well, they're unlikely to shed many tears. But in private or around people they're close with, they shed real tears during those tearjerker storylines. Scorpio can be a deeply emotional sign who processes their thoughts and feelings internally, and their connection to their own subconscious can mean that the best way for them to do so is by crying—even if it's over a movie.

LIBRA

Libra can be a big crier during movies because they tend to be a more emotional type. They're not normally the sign to cry at every film—Libras often have a specific genre or story trope that brings them to tears. Libras feel things deeply and genuinely, and this makes them cry frequently at movies. They can often be sensitive and empathetic signs, too, even if those qualities aren't always included as well-known Libra traits. This makes them likely to find at least one or two genres that will devastate them every time.

IF YOUR ZODIAC SIGN MADE THIS LIST, YOU'RE SUPER FORGETFUL

SAGITTARIUS

You've got a lot going on, Sagittarius, and your thoughts are usually not very organized. You can sometimes be a restless sign, which leads you to jump from one adventure to another. This also means that your thoughts can be scattered; you're not only focusing on a million different things at once, but you're changing your thoughts about each every second! To top all of this off, you also tend to be a multitasker. This means that you can sometimes be forgetful because you're doing too much at once—if you're packing your bag, reading something on your phone, and setting down your book, you're bound to forget where you put your book down later on.

PISCES

Your sign toes the line between dreams and reality. This also means that you're known for being a little forgetful. You may sometimes remember dreams as if they're real memories or just generally feel like the memories of your day are a little unclear sometimes. You have a lot going on when you commune with your inner consciousness; it's normal for you to be forgetful when your mind is processing your dreams, unconscious thoughts, and your conscious reality. Since you have so much to think about all at once, you often lose track of your thoughts (sometimes even in conversation).

AQUARIUS

You're so laser-focused on your work, you often end up forgetting other, smaller details about your life. You might struggle to remember what you had for dinner yesterday or where you put a small object. You might forget conversations or small details about people. To you, these aren't always major issues—you're a logical person, and you agree with your mind's decision to prioritize your major life projects and work. Still, it might be a good idea to write something down every now and again—your forgetfulness tends to come up most often with other people, whether it's a life event about someone you forgot or even a birthday.

DON'T CROSS THESE FOUR ZODIAC SIGNS— THEY'RE AMAZING AT SETTING BOUNDARIES

ARIES

No one should be surprised to see Aries on this list. After all, this sign is confident, a great leader, and never backs down from a challenge. They'd probably laugh at anybody who tried to overstep their boundaries (although let's face it, most people won't even bother trying).

Aries knows themselves well and has a good understanding of what they'll put up with. They're also good with other people, so they see through manipulation tactics easily—they always like to be one step ahead of the game, and that means understanding exactly what everyone is up to and why.

Even when they don't already have a specific set of boundaries in place for themselves, they're good at knowing exactly what they need in the moment. They're not the kind of sign to let things go or wait to address them until later. If something bothers them or if you overstep, they'll be sure to let you know… and make sure it doesn't happen again.

TAURUS

The sign of the stubborn bull isn't about to let anybody get past their boundaries unscathed. Taurus can get angry quickly—even if they seem like the sweetest, most docile person in the world—and they won't hesitate to defend their territory as soon as you cross a line.

Because Taurus loves routine and is a grounded sign, they know themselves well and have very clear boundaries for themselves on what they're comfortable with. Taurus's comfort zone can vary, but they'll make it clear when they feel their boundaries have been violated.

If you're lucky, Taurus will act calmly the first time you cross a line. But they hate being played with, so if anyone tries them twice, well, they're basically waving a bright red piece of cloth and asking to be charged.

LEO

Leo is an outspoken and generous sign. They have a large social circle and love being the center of attention. They're usually self-expressive and tend to be more extroverted. This makes it easier for them to speak up for themselves in a social setting—they're used to being in large groups, after all.

Because Leo is so charming and well-liked, they're not afraid of setting boundaries because they know it won't make them come across as being disagreeable. Anyone who tries to cross Leo in public will probably walk away feeling embarrassed and thoroughly shamed.

Leo has plenty of experience setting boundaries, and because they're a creative and expressive soul, they know themselves and their limits well. They're bold and often direct, and don't mind telling someone off if it means they can defend a boundary they've set for themselves. You'd be hard-pressed to find a Leo who won't speak up for themselves whenever they feel they need to.

AQUARIUS

Aquarius doesn't care about social norms, so they won't feel the need to bother with being polite when they think someone has overstepped. They're direct and say exactly what's on their mind—to the point of being blunt—and don't care whether or not it comes across nicely.

To Aquarius, if you're not going to respect them, you're not worth their time. They don't mind losing friends or acquaintances if it means being able to keep a firm boundary they've set for themselves.

Aquarius's loyalty extends to themselves and their values. They're a passionate sign that stands up for what they believe in—and if you thought that didn't extend to their personal boundaries, you thought wrong. Aquarius will halt anybody who so much as toes the line, and they won't care how strict or firm they have to be when it comes to protecting their space.

3 ZODIAC SIGNS WHO ARE MADE TO WORK REMOTELY

VIRGO

Virgo, your sign tends to prioritize efficiency and diligence. Not only is your work ethic completely trustworthy when it comes to working remotely, you may also find it easier to create a structured environment for yourself outside of the office. You appreciate environments that are customized to your preferences (and working from home may actually make you even more productive than usual). Because you don't struggle with discipline, you'd have no trouble building a productive schedule for yourself, even when you're not in the office. Mercury is your ruling planet, meaning your communication skills are just one of your many strong suits; this makes you perfect for keeping in touch with your teammates remotely.

SAGITTARIUS

Sagittarius, you're always on the go. You'd thrive at any job that gives you flexibility; your sign is dedicated to preserving your work-life balance and would appreciate the ability to set your own hours. You'd do best at remote work that's a little more asynchronous—though as a social sign, you also wouldn't mind checking in with your coworkers every now and again. As an optimist, you'd make virtual meetings collaborative and productive even from afar. Plus, you'd more than take advantage of the opportunity to set the perfect daily schedule for yourself and enjoy your time outside of work, too.

AQUARIUS

Your innovative thinking and natural flexibility means you're well-suited for a career outside of the office, Aquarius. Your sign enjoys working alone—once you're in the zone, you don't want to be disturbed. As a quirkier sign, you usually have your own routines when it comes to work; you'd appreciate the chance to work from the comfort of your own space, contributing new ideas and projects on your own time. Your sign also tends to have irregular circadian rhythms; you may be well-suited to remote work that can literally be done at any time, allowing you to get your work done late at night or early in the morning.

4 ZODIAC SIGNS WHO ARE MOST LIKELY TO CHOOSE THE WRONG CAREER PATH

CAPRICORN

Capricorn, you're very sure of yourself and are serious about your goals. In fact, you excel at a lot of things thanks to your sign's natural discipline and work ethic. This also means that you might lose sight of why you're accomplishing certain goals in the first place. Additionally, because you tend to be more of a logical than emotional sign, you might place much of the focus on finances and professional accomplishments when it comes to your work. This isn't necessarily a bad thing—it can seriously set you up for success in a way that your sign finds difficult to ignore. But also understand that being able to force yourself to be good at anything sometimes makes it hard to find the thing you're truly best at. You may also struggle with taking risks when it comes to your professional life, especially concerning your finances.

SAGITTARIUS

Sagittarius, you often put your personal freedom over your career. For your sign, it's difficult to imagine being tied down. You're a sign who would probably love a flexible schedule or remote work—you're also an adventurous person who likes to travel and doesn't enjoy most jobs that will keep you in the office year-round. This means you have a great perspective on work-life balance and a healthy professional career. Unfortunately, it also means that you can sometimes avoid putting any priority at all on your professional development. This can make you more likely than other signs to choose the wrong career path because you haven't explored all your options. Because you're also scared of taking professional risks due to your busy personal life, you may also avoid pursuing career paths you care about.

GEMINI

Gemini, you may struggle to commit to a professional path. You're always most excited by new things and new opportunities; for you, a professional decision could be made on a whim. When you follow what you're most interested in at the time, you gain a lot of different experiences—a major bonus for a curious sign like you. But this also prevents you from developing professionally in one field of interest—you get bored too easily to commit to developing a single sector of your career. Even worse, you might find yourself locked into a job you quickly become bored with because you tend to jump around so frequently.

AQUARIUS

Aquarius, you're not afraid to go against the status quo. You're also a brilliant innovator, which makes you likely to find success in many cases. But your sign is also likely to choose a career path that isn't quite right for you. Because of your rebellious streak, you sometimes lack realism when it comes to your professional pursuits. You easily excel at whatever you put your mind to, but you may also have a tendency to lock yourself into careers too quickly before you realize why you're not well-suited to them. Sometimes, you also dedicate yourself too much to something that isn't viable for you; you're willing to burn yourself out rather than jump ship when it's truly necessary.

3 ZODIAC SIGNS WHO ALWAYS SELF-SABOTAGE THEIR CAREERS

LEO

Leo, your sign is prone to self-sabotage in your professional life because you sometimes struggle with taking feedback. For you, your professional work is often an extension of your personality; you sometimes can't help but take feedback as a personal attack, even when it isn't. When you put your whole heart into your work and take pride in your accomplishments, your mind tries to shut down any outside criticism in order to protect your perception of yourself. In doing so, you also end up isolating yourself from professional connections and making yourself difficult to work with.

SAGITTARIUS

Sagittarius, it's your love of freedom that can prevent you from flourishing in your career. You feel bogged down by anything that has a deadline attached to it—for you, scheduled work can sometimes feel like a slog. Responsibility isn't always your sign's strong suit, and you're a sign who always wants to put your personal freedom and your life over your work. Still, Sagittarius, you struggle to find a balance that actually allows you to prioritize your career every once in a while. When you feel yourself getting overwhelmed in your professional life, you prefer to shut down and focus your energy towards your personal life instead. This act of self-sabotage often means you're left scrambling to salvage what you can of your work, leading you to repeat the cycle all over again later on.

GEMINI

Gemini, your professional self-sabotage is truly an accident. You're a big fan of starting new projects—your mind wants constant entertainment for its endless curiosity, and you can't help but be much more interested in new projects than old ones. Your work on a new project tends to be more dedicated and intense than on old ones, and sometimes your sign's attempts to bounce around from commitment to commitment means nothing ends up getting done. You want to be successful at everything and love balancing dozens of personal and professional projects on top of each other, but this also means that it's usually right when your career is going well that you start accidentally sabotaging all of your hard work.

HOW YOU WOULD DIE ON THE 1974 OREGON TRAIL GAME, BASED ON YOUR ZODIAC SIGN

ARIES: ATTACKED BY WILD ANIMALS

Aries, your bold and adventurous spirit would lead you to take risks on The Oregon Trail—you'll do anything to avoid having to buy food on the way, won't you? Unfortunately, your daring attitude would result in a fatal encounter with wild animals. Your fearless nature, always ready for a challenge, would sadly be your downfall in the face of the great wilderness.

TAURUS: DROWNING WHILE CROSSING A RIVER

Taurus, your preference for the direct approach would see you attempting to ford every river you come across (let's face it, we've all been there). Your determination is admirable, but your stubbornness would be your downfall—and it would be the downfall of the rest of your traveling party, too. Well, Taurus, you can't say you didn't try.

GEMINI: A FEVER

Gemini, you're a social and curious sign, and you like to look out for the other members in your party. Unfortunately, your wide social circle can get the best of you on the Oregon Trail, where diseases spread quickly. You'd be most likely to die of a fever; easily spread but not easily treatable when you're far away from camp. You'd probably encourage the rest of your party to push on anyway—you're just heroic like that.

CANCER: ACCIDENTAL GUNSHOT

Cancer, your protective instincts might lead you to be overly cautious and trigger-happy, especially when it comes to defending your wagon from threats. Strong defense comes with its own risks, though, and your sensitive soul isn't always the fightin' type. Too bad your wagon didn't learn more about gun safety beforehand.

LEO: SNAKE BITE

Leo, your dramatic and courageous nature would likely lead you to underestimate the vast wilderness on your journey. Your desire to forge ahead—even without a healthy dose of precaution—would probably lead you to succumb to a fatal snake bite. What a way to go out.

VIRGO: TYPHOID FEVER

Virgo, your meticulous planning and concern for details might ironically lead to your downfall through typhoid fever. Despite your efforts to maintain cleanliness and order, the harsh conditions of the trail and limited resources can still lead to unpredictable illness, demonstrating that sometimes even the best-laid Oregon Trail journeys can still end in disaster.

LIBRA: DYSENTERY

Libra, your desire for balance and harmony might be disrupted on the Oregon Trail by the dreaded dysentery. Let's face it, who hasn't died of dysentery on the Oregon Trail? Your conflict-solving efforts to keep everyone well-fed and happy won't last long with the trail's contaminated food and water sources.

SCORPIO: A BROKEN LEG

Scorpio, you're a driven and focused sign, and you'd probably be great at trying your hand on the Oregon Trail. But your determination doesn't mean you can avoid every pitfall on the trail. You're a strategic planner who likes to calculate your next move; you'd probably try to see if you can make it just a little longer without treating your broken leg (after all, it costs a lot of time). Alas, this would only result in a relatively tame death tally for you.

SAGITTARIUS: STARVATION

Sagittarius, your sense of adventure would help you feel at home on the trail, but it would probably also lead to overconfidence in your ability to find food and resources. This could lead you to forge ahead even when you're running low on resources (who wants to spend time stopping along the trail, anyway?). You (and the rest of your wagon) would likely meet their untimely ends due to lack of food.

CAPRICORN: EXHAUSTION

Capricorn, your hardworking and ambitious approach would have you pushing yourself and your party to the limits on The Oregon Trail. Your goal is to achieve the highest score, and you'll stop at nothing to get there. This relentless drive will probably lead you to die of exhaustion more often than not. Your dedication to reaching your destination might cause you to ignore the needs of your party until it's too late.

AQUARIUS: CHOLERA

Aquarius, your innovative spirit and tendency to think outside the box might not always translate well to the practicalities of retro trail life. An unexpected outbreak of cholera could catch you off guard, leading to a swift and unforeseen demise. This is one of those unlucky events that even your hard-working, innovative self can't defend against.

PISCES: DROWNING IN A FLASH FLOOD

Pisces, your dreamy and sometimes absent-minded nature would definitely result in a lack of awareness about the weather. Your sign would be most likely to succumb to a sudden flash flood—imagine you're hanging out by a riverbank, not paying too much attention to your surroundings, and suddenly your wagon is afloat. At least your water sign is given a tragically poetic ending.

TRAVEL & ADVENTURE

For planning your next adventure.

WHICH WORLD WONDER YOU MUST SEE BEFORE YOU DIE, BASED ON YOUR ZODIAC SIGN

ARIES

Aries, your adventurous and determined nature aligns perfectly with the towering majesty of Mount Everest. Just as you are always striving to reach new heights and take on challenges head-first, Everest represents the ultimate challenge and symbol of strength. Your bold and ambitious spirit finds its reflection in the courageous climbers who dare to face the world's highest peak.

TAURUS

Taurus, you are grounded and have a deep appreciation for beauty and stability, much like the Great Barrier Reef. Your love for time spent in nature and natural beauty resonates with the vibrant colors and rich biodiversity of this reef. This underwater marvel is also a testament to the beauty and resilience of nature, qualities that you hold dear.

GEMINI

Gemini, your sign has a dual nature and is ruled by Mercury, making you adaptable and social. You'll find a celestial counterpart in the Northern Lights. This ethereal light show is ever-changing and filled with a multitude of colors, reflecting your multifaceted personality and your ability to adapt to different situations with grace and charm.

Just as you enjoy many different hobbies and social circles, the Northern Lights are visible from many places.

CANCER

Cancer, you're an emotional sign ruled by the Moon, making you closely aligned with the ebb and flow of the tides. These qualities are mirrored in the almost-magical healing waters of the Dead Sea. Just as you provide comfort and care to those around you, the Dead Sea offers therapeutic qualities and a sense of tranquility. You're an intuitive and sentimental sign, so you'll find comfort in this serene natural wonder.

LEO

Leo, your vibrant and vivacious personality requires a wonder of the world just as brilliant as you are. Your traits are echoed in the lush and bustling life of the Amazon Rainforest. Like you, the Amazon is full of life, color, and even a sense of royalty. Your natural leadership (and your bold, colorful life) finds a parallel in the dynamic ecosystem of this magnificent jungle.

VIRGO

Virgo, your practical, meticulous nature and your appreciation for hard work align with the Great Wall of China. Just as you strive for perfection and order, the Great Wall stands as a testament to meticulous craftsmanship and enduring strength, qualities you hold in high regard. Like you, the Great Wall is the pinnacle of organization, hard work, and patience.

LIBRA

Libra, you're well-known for loving beauty, balance, and harmony; this side of you is encapsulated in the breathtaking island of Santorini. Your diplomatic and charming personality aligns with the welcoming vibes and serene beauty of the island. With its stunning sunsets, blindingly white buildings, and crystal-clear waters, Santorini exudes an exacting balance of romance and aesthetics.

SCORPIO

Scorpio, your intense and transformative nature finds a match in the mysterious depths of the Grand Canyon. Like you, the Grand Canyon holds layers of complexity and hidden wonders, revealing its secrets only to those who dare to delve deep. Your passion and determination resonate with the relentless shaping forces that created this awe-inspiring landscape.

SAGITTARIUS

Sagittarius, you harbor an obvious love for adventure and freedom. You align most with the wide-open spaces of the Serengeti. This landscape is wild, free, and full of opportunities for exploration and adventure—just as you like it. You're both an optimistic and philosophical soul, and you'll find a kindred spirit in the timeless cycle of life that plays out across these vast plains.

CAPRICORN

Capricorn, your disciplined, ambitious nature and respect for tradition and history fit with the monumental grandeur of Mount Rushmore. Your practical and responsible side is sure to find inspiration in the precision and dedication that went into creating this iconic sculpture. This landmark stands as a testament to hard work, determination, and reverence for the past—and those are three things you can definitely appreciate.

AQUARIUS

Aquarius, your perfect match can be found in the unique biodiversity and conservation efforts of the Galápagos Islands. These islands are a hub of originality, hosting an array of species found nowhere else on Earth. Your humanitarian qualities will appreciate how the Galápagos stand as a testament to the beauty and importance of maintaining our planet's natural diversity.

PISCES

Pisces, your connection to your ruling planet, Neptune, makes you both mystical and compassionate. You'll find your reflection in the deep, serene waters of the Great Blue Hole. This underwater sinkhole is mysterious, captivating, and holds hidden depths; your ruling planet, Neptune, reflects similar qualities onto your sign. You're intuitive and empathetic, meaning you're likely to find a sense of calm in the tranquility of this aquatic wonder.

HERE'S YOUR WEIRD SIDE HUSTLE IDEA, BASED ON YOUR ZODIAC SIGN

ARIES: MOTIVATIONAL SPEAKER

You're a leader, Aries, and a good one at that. You're confident, charismatic, and everyone seems to like you right away. Now's your chance to establish yourself as a motivational speaker—someone who gets paid to teach crowds of people all about your field of expertise. Whether you want to help people get the most out of their relationship or even start their own business, all you need to get started is a platform of your own to advertise your skills on.

TAURUS: PLANT NURSE

As an earth sign with the ruling planet Venus, your sign is likely to have a serious green thumb. This means that you should try advertising yourself as a dedicated plant nurse. You're looking for anyone who is either bad with plants and needs regular care, or anyone who has a plant in poor condition they want nursed back to health. You can even expand your services to gardening and garden designing, plant propagation, and more.

GEMINI: TANDEM BIKE TOUR GUIDE

Ever wanted to make a friend or two through your side hustle? What about showing off your favorite places and giving an educational tour while you work? Tandem bike tours involve you, a tandem bike, and one (or two, or three) other person(s), depending on how many seats your bike has. Together, all of you will take a scenic bike tour throughout a city, countryside, or biking trail with you as the guide. This makes it easier for tourists to enjoy the scenery without having to worry about steering or navigating.

CANCER: PROFESSIONAL FRIEND

Did you know that you can get paid to be a professional friend? Maybe it sounds weird, but this side hustle is actually getting pretty serious. It first began in Japan, with apps designed to help users find a designated friend that they can bring with them to activities they don't have someone to go to with. Not only will you get paid to be someone's friend for a day, you'll also get to do fun activities with them—amusement parks, cafe visits, city tours, and more.

LEO: STOCK IMAGE MODELING

You're usually one to be the star of the show, Leo, and what better way to do it than by being a model? A stock image model, of course—which is arguably even more fun. You'll be paid to take professional photos in a variety of settings, often acting out scenes or emotions for the camera. After that, you might find yourself on websites, advertisements, or even billboards.

VIRGO: COUPON BLOGGER

Have you ever wanted to have a negative grocery bill and make the store pay you? Maybe you just enjoy keeping a good eye on deals near you (even if you have to go to 3 different stores to make it work). Coupon blogging is a lucrative practice, and it pays. All you'd need to do is post your coupon findings online for anyone to stumble across. You'll rake in cash from companies looking to advertise deals on your website—and you'll get to save yourself plenty of money on groceries and home goods, too.

LIBRA: ONLINE JUROR

You can exercise your judicial mindset from the comfort of your own home if you choose to be an online juror as a side hustle, Libra. You'll simply sign up with a legal website that needs jurors to review mock cases. Then, you can assign yourself cases to attend virtually as a paid juror—which certainly beats jury duty.

SCORPIO: HAUNTED HOUSE ACTOR

The best part about your side hustle is that you don't have to worry about doing it all year long. Training will usually start in July or August, and most haunted houses will run from September through the end of October—or for even less time. Since your sign is most likely to be a fan of horror, a lover of the autumn season (and of Halloween), and great with mysteries, signing up to be a haunted house actor is right up your alley.

SAGITTARIUS: WILDERNESS COOKING VLOGGER

Have you ever admired a food influencer on social media for how beautiful their dishes look? Or maybe you're busy enjoying watching people camping outside and showing off their tent setups. Now, you can combine both of these arts into one by becoming a wilderness food influencer. These niche accounts film themselves cooking (and sometimes even catching and foraging) food outdoors, often using river water, rocks, and campfires to cook elaborate dishes. Since you love the outdoors, don't mind a bit of isolation, and enjoy learning new things, your ideal side hustle is making money off of your wilderness social media channel.

CAPRICORN: SELLING SOCIAL MEDIA ACCOUNTS

Did you know that social media accounts with 1,000 or more followers can actually sell for cold, hard cash? Most accounts worth selling will have over 5,000 followers, and you can sell these accounts for at least $100 or more. If you amass 100,000 followers or more, you might even be able to sell your account for thousands of dollars. Best of all, you can also make money as you gain followers through the accounts you're preparing to sell. You're a hard worker, highly organized, and would probably find the rush to gain as many followers as possible exciting.

AQUARIUS: MICROGREEN GROWER

There's money to be made at the farmer's market, Aquarius, and it's your turn to take advantage of it. As a humanitarian sign, you'd appreciate the chance to do something good for the environment and for your bank account. Growing microgreens is a lucrative side hustle because you won't need much space to do it. Microgreens are just very young vegetables and herbs, usually harvested within a week or two of germinating. They can often sell for some serious cash, and you'll only need a spot at a farmer's market to get started selling them yourself.

PISCES: LIVE ART MODEL

As a creative soul, you likely already have some untapped connections to studios that need live models. You'll also get to connect with other artists—and if your main job is in a creative field, it's good to have an unrelated side hustle so you can give your brain a break. Plus, you're already a natural daydreamer, which means you'll have more than enough time to let your brain run free and get paid to do so. You'll definitely enjoy the (often hefty) paycheck for a few hours of daydreaming.

YOU SHOULD TAKE THESE ZODIAC SIGNS ON A ROAD TRIP

SAGITTARIUS

Ever the optimist, Sagittarius is a good person to have along on a road trip adventure. They're usually well-prepared given their experience with travel, and they'll be so excited about the journey they'll never bother asking, "Are we there yet?" You might have to deal with them constantly finding spontaneous stops along the way they want to visit, but at the very least, you'll have your own impromptu tour guide making the experience more fun for whoever else you've chosen to take along with you.

VIRGO

There's something about Virgo that makes them handy to have along on any kind of trip (yes, it's the fact that they're super organized). Need a travel planner with a full itinerary? Wondering what you should pack? Trying to map out the most efficient route that compromises time and fuel? Trying to negotiate the stops you'll actually be stopping at? Virgo probably already has all of these things handled…and more. Just know that they prefer to plan things out well in advance, so they may be a little miffed if you ignore their thought-out itinerary too many times.

CANCER

Because Cancer is so good at caring for others, they're a genuinely enjoyable sign to have along on a road trip. They're good at keeping things calm within the group and preparing in advance for any emergencies that might happen along the way. As a sensitive soul, they're not likely to involve themselves in arguments or fall victim to the road trip blues. They place empathy and care above all, which makes them a good person to have around when you're stuck in close quarters with a lot of people for a long time.

LIBRA

As the natural mediator of any group, Libra is a perfect person to add to your car for a long road trip. They're key for stopping fights from breaking out and making sure everyone knows how to compromise. Whether they're preventing someone from getting their feelings hurt over a missed stop or are just busy reminding everyone to get some sleep, they're sure to be on their game to keep tensions from rising well in advance. If you're hoping to plan an ultimate road trip without a single disagreement, it's Libra you'll want to have in the backseat.

PICK YOUR ZODIAC SIGN AND GET AN EASY WEEKEND ACTIVITY

ARIES: ROCK CLIMBING

You don't need to spend a ton of time learning the ropes (literally) or venturing outside to make rock climbing an easy weekend activity. Just walk into a gym near you and hop on the wall. To go bouldering, you won't need any instruction at all—it's fun, it's thrilling, and it's an activity you'll definitely enjoy. If you're more interested in rock climbing (with ropes), you can learn the skill in a weekend by simply having a staff member belay you in a private rock climbing session. Though you might wish this activity could last all day, there's no one who isn't wiped out after a two or three hour session.

TAURUS: VISITING A BOTANICAL GARDEN

You'll love the opportunity to be surrounded by nature in a relaxed, calming environment. There's no pressure to reach a particular destination as with hiking, and the pace tends to be even calmer than just going for a walk. You'll be given plenty of opportunities to sit and enjoy the view, which will help relax and inspire your mind. Botanical gardens are a refreshing yet simple weekend activity—you can spend just a half hour in one or the entire day.

GEMINI: ROLLER BLADING

More than just a way to get some cardio in, rollerblading is a great way to have fun with friends (or make some new ones). From skating along to your favorite songs to participating in skating games, spending a few hours of your weekend at the rink is a fun activity whether you're with a group or on your own. Best of all, it's relatively easy to pick up, so if you've never been before, you won't need to dedicate tons of time to learning to skate.

CANCER: POTTERY CLASS

Whether you're interested in pottery painting or forming the entire thing yourself, a pottery class is a great activity for a creative sign like you, Cancer. It's a good way to burn off some steam during the weekend and enjoy a quiet day to yourself or some quality time with those close to you. It's often important to you to have a sentimental souvenir of memories or times that are important to you—what better way to save a memory than by leaving class with a handcrafted piece of pottery?

LEO: OPEN MIC NIGHT

Whether you're looking to perform something yourself or just watch others…Well, let's face it, Leo, you're going to want to perform. Not only does this give you a way to enjoy performing some of your hobbies for others, it can even help to keep you accountable with goals you set for yourself. You're rarely afraid to put yourself out there, and an open mic night is a fun way to enjoy the spotlight for a few minutes, whether it be in front of friends or total strangers. Best of all, you'll have a great story to tell the office come Monday…

VIRGO: COOKING CLASS

As someone who likes to be precise and is invested in their daily schedule, a cooking class is perfect for you, Virgo. Not only can you learn more about cooking no matter your level—whether you're looking for beginner classes or trying to make more advanced dishes—you can focus on whatever cuisine and skill you're trying to learn. This can help with anything from impressing your friends with your baking skills to incorporating meal prepping into your efficient weekly schedule. Plus, you can easily learn a skill in just one class, making it a valuable weekend activity.

LIBRA: DANCING

Whether you head to a bar with live music, go clubbing, or take a dance class, you might be surprised to know that dancing is a great weekend activity for a Libra. As a sociable and graceful sign, dancing will be relatively easy for you to pull off. Your ruling sign, Venus, means that you love all things aesthetic—you might opt to learn some ballet, go salsa dancing, or just head to the nearest studio that lets you put on stylish clothing to dance in. It's also a fantastic idea for a romantic date night, which you might appreciate. You can also pull a large group together to spend a dressed-up night out.

SCORPIO: RAGE ROOM

You're very in tune with your inner self, Scorpio. You probably already have a good routine for managing your emotions and destressing on the weekends. But have you ever considered heading to a rage room for a therapeutic session of smashing glass and throwing things around? You can bring a group of friends with you or head in for a session alone, and most sessions will only take around an hour or less of your time. Though a rage room might sound like a strange activity, it can be a beneficial way of processing emotions, especially pent-up ones. Or maybe you just want to break stuff with your friends, who knows. You have remarkable self-control, so it can be fun for you to let loose sometimes.

SAGITTARIUS: TRIVIA NIGHT

You always love learning something new, Sagittarius, and are known to be a wise sign. Because your interests tend to be so varied, you might be a secret trivia ace without even knowing it. But regardless of whether or not the trivia questions are geared towards your specialities, you'll still have a fun night. Bring along a group of friends or find a table to join in with—at the very least, you'll probably pick up a few fun facts to wow others with later on.

CAPRICORN: MYSTERY BOX

If you're looking for a fun night with friends, bonding time with family, or a fun date idea for your partner, a mystery box is for you—and yes, you can also complete them solo (fewer arguments that way, right?). If you've never encountered mystery boxes before, they're essentially a mystery (usually a murder) in a box that can be solved within a few hours. The box will contain everything you need to solve the mystery—filled with letters from characters, documents, police reports, items from the scene of the crime, and a wide list of suspects. It's up to you to solve the story yourself (or in a group). This is the perfect weekend night activity for a disciplined, driven person like yourself.

AQUARIUS: ARCADE

If you're looking for a way to blow off some steam, relax, and maybe even win some prizes, the arcade is for you. It's a little nostalgic, offers plenty of different activities to try, and is a great place to go with friends. Knowing your sign, you'll probably figure out a way to cheat the system and rack up some serious tickets on a single game.

PISCES: VISITING A FARMER'S MARKET

A farmer's market is the perfect weekend activity for you, Pisces. It gives you plenty of flexibility on where you want to go and how long you want to spend there—and the pieces you find might even inspire some creativity of your own. It's both practical and exciting, whether you're looking to find unique purchases or just stock up on fresh groceries. Since you're also a hopeless romantic, it can be a seriously adorable idea for a date. You're also likely to find art pieces you connect to and live music to enjoy throughout the day, making it perfect for a creative and imaginative sign like yourself.

YOU SHOULD BRING THESE 3 ZODIAC SIGNS ON YOUR NEXT CAMPING TRIP

SAGITTARIUS

This sign is most likely to have spent a lot of time outdoors. They tend to be more adventurous—especially when those adventures involve nature—and are highly independent and resourceful. They're handy to have if you need a few extra wilderness survival skills or just want an optimist on your side if things go wrong. Sagittarius is also a free spirit, so you won't get sick of having them hang around on long trips.

VIRGO

Virgo is uber-organized and prepared for everything. They get along well with nature and generally find the great outdoors to be calming. They're also big on peace and quiet, so they'd prefer to go somewhere more isolated for a true vacation. Virgo is definitely going to catch at least ten essential items you left off your packing list, and they're bound to have endless backup supplies in case someone needs a first-aid kit, extra food, or more water. You definitely won't have to worry about taking care of Virgo out in the woods—they know what they're doing.

TAURUS

The sign of the bull is known for being extremely grounded and practical. They're highly responsible and resourceful, making them good at preparing for anything and staying calm in stressful situations. They're a handy person to have on your camping team—not only do they genuinely enjoy being out in nature, they're also good at organizing a group and figuring out exactly what needs to be done. They'll have your campsite set up in a flash—and even better, this sign tends to be amazing at cooking, too.

THESE 4 ZODIAC SIGNS ARE RESTLESS RIGHT NOW. HERE'S WHAT THEY SHOULD DO

LIBRA

Libra, you're feeling at odds with yourself right now. Either you're unsure of the path you're taking or you just don't have enough to do. The best thing you can do for yourself right now is to design a better schedule. You might want to wake up earlier, get outside more, or find an activity (volunteering, a hobby, visiting family) that makes you feel good about yourself. Not only will this give you a bigger purpose with your restless energy, it might help you to redefine your values and goals. Plus, if the biggest problem is that your days are empty, creating a set schedule for yourself will help you to fill them quickly.

CAPRICORN

It's probably the season that has you feeling full of energy. You typically plow onwards with your work at the same speed all year, but something in the air has you feeling a little more restless than usual. For you, Capricorn, the key isn't to work more, but to plan something that will give your mind a break. You should try to find something that will get you out of the house and moving around—one potential roadblock for you right now is that your mind has been hard at work, but your body feels restless and full of energy. Look for summer festivals or events near you, theme parks, hiking trips, street fairs, or food trucks you can visit. Walk around, get some fresh air, and take a break from the endless grind for a while.

TAURUS

As an earth sign, you're very in-tune with nature and the energy of the earth. Right now, with everything full of life, you're probably feeling a sudden energy spike. Your mind is used to having a set routine that you follow, and your energy levels have adapted to that routine—after all, for you, structure is everything. But now that a new season is here, you're suddenly feeling more restless than usual, and your regular routine won't cut it. Your body and mind will adapt soon, but for now, you need to add something that helps bring your energy levels back down. Since you're a sign that doesn't like to change things up too much (and will probably want to add something reliable to your regular schedule), exercise is your best bet. Opt for something outdoors—running, biking, swimming—or something you can add to a stable home schedule—yoga, weightlifting, stretching, short workouts.

SAGITTARIUS

It's probably no surprise to you that you're feeling a little out of sorts if you have a lot of extra energy to spend. Naturally, the best thing for you to do is plan a kind of outdoor adventure that will help you use up that extra energy. If it's feasible for you, traveling is always a good way to spend part of your summer. Road trips, destination vacations, or even some time off to travel around your hometown are all good ways to get your extra energy out. As a sign who loves the outdoors, you may also opt to go hiking, trail running, or camping. Planning on staying close to home? Physical activities to use up your energy are best. Do some gardening or yard work, wash your car, clean your roof, move some furniture—you'll feel better in no time.

PICK YOUR ZODIAC SIGN AND GET AN ADVENTURE TO HAVE THIS YEAR

ARIES: WHITE-WATER RAFTING

Aries, you've got more courage than most other zodiac signs. Why not take yourself (and maybe some backup) on a white-water rafting trip? Not only will you get the chance to get outdoors and enjoy an extra-unique workout, you'll also get that adrenaline rush your sign loves to look for. Plus, you'll get to brag to your friends about how adventurous you are.

TAURUS: VISITING A NATIONAL PARK

Taurus, you sometimes struggle to get out of your comfort zone, but you also enjoy getting out into nature. What better way to explore at your own pace than by visiting a national park? Whether you want to do a casual day trip and enjoy creature comforts at a nearby hotel or get out in the wilderness with a solo camping trip, national parks give you more flexibility so you can enjoy a cozier adventure.

GEMINI: OPEN MIC NIGHT

Gemini, you're a social sign who's big on trying new things—why not gather up your friends and head to an open mic night? You can show off your talents and enjoy a night out in your area—you might even meet some new connections while you're at it. Whether you're interested in a poetry reading or stand up comedy, public speaking is something your sign tends to excel at thanks to your ruling planet Mercury.

LEO: VISITING A HISTORICAL THEATER

You're a creative sign, Leo, and you've probably heard that you're a bit of a drama queen, too. Why not take the opportunity to travel to a historical theater and get to see a show at the same time? Maybe you want to go big and visit the recreation of Shakespeare's Globe—or maybe you just want to visit the fanciest theater in your area to catch a few live performances. Either way, a theater with detailed architecture and exciting performances is your best bet for adventuring this year.

VIRGO: BOTANICAL GARDEN VISIT

For you, there's no better adventure than a day exploring a tranquil botanical garden—you could even take the opportunity to make a full trip of it and head for some of the biggest gardens in the world. Your attention to detail and your green thumb will make this the perfect trip for you, Virgo—you might even get some inspiration for your own plant collection.

LIBRA: COUNTRYSIDE B&B RETREAT

Libra, as a social sign who likes to relax every once in a while, you'd probably enjoy a quaint weekend away in the countryside. You're someone who appreciates beauty in natural environments (and your mood tends to be greatly affected by your surroundings). For a sign who often struggles with burnout, some time spent in peace and quiet (with all your meals taken care of for you) could be the perfect adventure for you this year.

SCORPIO: SPELUNKING

You should probably hire a guide for this one, Scorpio. With your sign's interest in the dark and macabre, spelunking could be an interesting adventure combo for you. Not only will it give you the opportunity to flex your adventuring skills, you'll also get to learn a lot about the natural history of an area and visit places most people have never ventured before. You'd probably be the kind of person to learn about spelunking horror stories to regale your tour group with, right?

SAGITTARIUS: BACKPACKING TRIP

Whenever you need to find yourself, Sagittarius, you prefer to do it alone—like, seriously alone. You're a big fan of heading out into nature to clear your head, and a backpacking trip is the perfect 2024 adventure for you. Not only do you get to choose the terrain, length, and style of your trip, it will also give you the opportunity to reflect on your year so far before it's over. You usually find yourself coming out of the woods with a better understanding of yourself—the longer the better, right Sagittarius?

CAPRICORN: SAILING EXPEDITION

Grab your Dramamine, Capricorn—you should head on a sailing expedition at some point this year. You enjoy accomplishing things that most other people wouldn't be able to (and you always like to add a new skill to your belt). For you, an adventure isn't an adventure if you don't accomplish a goal while you're at it. Learning to sail or staging an expedition of your own would give you a serious goal (and great memories to look back on)—as long as you get your sea legs quickly, of course.

AQUARIUS: STARGAZING TOUR

Did you know that your sign is most likely to have a fascination with astronomy, Aquarius? Heading out and away from any light pollution for a stargazing tour would be a fantastic 2024 adventure for you. Opting for a guided tour could give you more time to learn how to navigate the constellations and maybe even get to see a few planets up close and personal. You should opt for a trip that allows you to see (and learn about) the most populated night sky possible.

PISCES: WELLNESS RETREAT

Pisces, your sign tends to be a little more spiritual—and you're also big on self-care and creativity. A wellness retreat would be an adventure that leaves you refreshed, energized, and with new insights (and hopefully some new inspiration, too). Going on a wellness retreat adventure leaves you with plenty of options to pick from, whether you want physical activities like yoga and hiking or one that gives you time for physical self-care like meditation and spa days.

ASTROLOGICAL EVENTS & HOLIDAYS

These astrological events can supercharge your life.

THE IDEAL TAROT CARDS TO DRAW FOR THE NEW YEAR

THE FOOL

The Fool comes to those who will receive new beginnings. He advises you to leap into the unknown and accept every opportunity that comes your way. If there's a project you've been considering launching or an idea you can't help but want to get started on, the Fool advises you to go for it.

The Fool is on an adventure that he goes into blindly, but it is one that will end positively. Keep your eyes open for new opportunities in the new year. A new, positive chapter of your life will begin shortly.

THE STAR

The Star is all about hope. It gives new energy to its recipients and indicates that your efforts will soon see you rewarded. The Star is known by many to represent the 'light at the end of the tunnel'; it promises that the future is bright and that you will soon be able to celebrate new successes.

The Star is also a good card to receive in relation to healing. If you've been reflecting on the past year and working on healing yourself to enter the new year with new intentions, the Star is a wonderful indication that you've been successful in doing so. The Star promises a year full of inner healing, peace, and health.

THE LOVERS

If you receive this card during New Year's, it could indicate that you're going to find love in the new year. If you're already in a relationship and have pulled this card, congratulations—this card appears to those who are in stable, healthy relationships. It might just mean you've found your soulmate.

Regardless, the Lovers promise a joyous new year to all who pull it. If you find yourself drawing the Lovers card on the day of the new year (or just before it begins), you're bound to have significant luck in love during the new year. Expect new relationships to spark or your current relationship to flourish in ways you've never seen before.

THE SUN

The Sun symbolizes success. If you've been wondering where the new year will take you, the Sun card is a positive card to receive. It means that your new year will be abundant, that you will achieve success in your endeavors, and that you will find happiness. Generally, the Sun card is known to be an extremely positive tarot card. It brings new energy, positive growth, and great happiness to those who draw it.

THESE TAROT CARDS WILL GUIDE YOU THROUGH SAGITTARIUS SEASON

Sagittarius season is all about exploration and adventure. You're likely to feel more optimistic, pursue new goals, and spend time with family and friends. You may feel a call to travel—and you might even find yourself reassessing your ambitions.

Throughout the season, there are two tarot cards you're more likely to pull than usual. These cards both relate to Sagittarius—so there's no surprise that you'll be seeing more of them during Sagittarius's time of year. They can help to guide you through the new emotions and experiences you're gaining during Sagittarius season. Make sure you know what they mean so you're prepared when you see them more frequently this month.

TEMPERANCE

Temperance is the card that is associated with Sagittarius. It is all about finding balance—both within yourself and throughout the rest of your life, too. It may indicate that you have achieved a harmonious relationship, that you have perfected your work-life balance, or that you feel that your inner self is at peace.

Additionally, Temperance can indicate a part of your life where you might need to find more balance. If you are asking your tarot deck a specific question, Temperance might indicate that there is a middle ground you should seek. This could relate to new opportunities you've been offered or new goals you've set for yourself.

During Sagittarius season, where many signs will feel the call to adventure and an interest in exploration, Temperance is a reminder to find balance in all things. Venture ahead with an open mind, but don't overdo anything in your life.

THE WHEEL OF FORTUNE

Jupiter is Sagittarius's ruling planet. Jupiter oversees the Temperance card, as both are connected to Sagittarius. However, Jupiter on its own is also heavily related to the Wheel of Fortune. This means that this card can be a useful guide during Sagittarius season.

If you pull this card, it indicates that a new cycle in your life is taking place. It is known to mean that a person's fortune must change significantly throughout the course of their life. If you have been down on your luck lately, you might find yourself uplifted by a new opportunity or sudden change. The Wheel of Fortune might also indicate that it is time for an upheaval in your life; one that you may not like, but that will eventually reveal its own blessings.

Look out for this card appearing more often than usual during Sagittarius season. This does not necessarily mean that you will experience continuous enormous shifts in your life, but rather that one single shift throughout this season is taking place for you. It could also simply indicate extreme luck or fortune; a simpler interpretation for those who receive it commonly this month.

IF YOU WANT TO SUPERCHARGE YOUR INTUITION, READ TAROT DURING THE COLD MOON

The end of the year has a finality that can be immensely important to tarot readers, regardless of whether or not tarot is a spiritual practice for you. As the year draws to a close, it's important to reflect on the successes and goals you've achieved this year. Communing with your inner self with the help of your tarot deck can provide you with significant insights to guide you throughout the new year.

Combining this end-of-year spirit with the final full Moon of the year—also known as a Cold Moon—can supercharge your tarot deck with positive energy. Many believe that the light of the full Moon has spiritual powers, and that doesn't just apply to witchcraft or crystals; you can cleanse your tarot deck under the light of the full Moon, too. But if you don't believe in cleansing, you might just want to read tarot on the final full moon of the year instead.

The full Moon can give both you and your deck extra positive energy, which can help you feel more aligned with your deck. You might feel more intuitive on this day as well, thanks to the moon's organic energies; this can aid you in understanding and interpreting the cards you pull more clearly.

If you receive certain cards related to the Moon on the Cold Moon—such as the Moon card or the High Priestess—know that they may have an additional meaning attached to them.

They may intend to advise on inner reflection, to help power your intuition, or just to bless you with new energy as the year wraps up.

The moon is often said to be related to the mind and to intuition. This makes the day of the Cold Moon the best day to ask complex questions of your tarot deck or to seek extended guidance from it. You may find it much easier to interpret the cards than usual. You might also be able to come up with multiple ways each card applies to your life.

The final full moon of the year is also a fantastic day to practice new spreads or ask your tarot deck for continued advice by pulling cards after you have received your initial spread. This can help you decipher even more about the cards, further honing your energy and intuition.

HERE ARE 4 LUCKY ZODIAC SIGNS THAT WILL TRULY BLOSSOM THIS SUMMER

LEO

Leo, with the summer Sun in full swing, you're bound to come into your most joyous, generous, and fun personality. You're an optimist at heart and also a deeply social sign—with the warm weather comes plenty of opportunities for social engagement and good vibes. Best of all, this summer is likely to bring you plenty of creative inspiration and opportunities, helping your passions and career to flourish along with your vibrant, loving personality.

SAGITTARIUS

You're always at your best when there are plenty of opportunities for adventure around, and summer is the time like no other for you to bloom into your best self. As the most optimistic zodiac sign, your positivity blossoms during the summer season. You're also presented with ways to get outdoors and be active, which helps boost your productivity along with your mood. By reconnecting with nature and spending plenty of time in the sun, there's no doubt you'll feel like your best self this season.

TAURUS

As an earth sign, your sign is highly connected to nature. This brings you abundance in your personal life, comfort, and positive energy when the rest of the world is in bloom. With summer in full swing, you'll feel warm, relaxed, and even happier than usual. This will give you more ways to take joy and pride in your hobbies and your career, and it will also present you with the chance to reconnect with nature and feel more grounded with yourself. Watching your indoor or outdoor plants come into full bloom alongside yourself this summer is the reward your sign deserves.

VIRGO

This summer, you're likely to both feel more productive and have more time on your hands for personal projects, Virgo. Whether you want to redecorate your home, take on DIY projects, or just dedicate more of your schedule to your passions, summer is a great opportunity for you to do so. As a somewhat social sign, you're likely to feel more extroverted with the good weather, giving you the chance to boost your mood by meeting others outside and scheduling activities that interest you.

THESE TAROT CARDS WILL BOOST YOUR PRODUCTIVITY DURING CAPRICORN SEASON

THE DEVIL

You might be surprised to learn that the Devil is Capricorn's tarot card. So, starting on December 22nd, you need to keep an eye out for this card in your readings. Despite its name, it's not an intrinsically bad card; in fact, it can be positive.

For one, the Devil card reminds you to pursue your passions. It wants you to prioritize the things you love, your hobbies, and your career. It also encourages you to find balance within your life; to not chase something (or someone) to such an extent that your life loses all other purpose.

The Devil can also appear as a reminder that something in your life needs to change. You may find the Devil when you are feeling stuck or trapped by your life circumstances; the Devil is telling you that you have the power to change them, but that you must determinedly take matters into your own hands in order to escape. As a zodiac sign who is constantly moving forward with determination, Capricorn would most certainly approve.

THE WORLD

This card is said to be ruled by Saturn, which is also Capricorn's ruling planet. It's another card to look out for during Capricorn season, as it may have something to tell you during the season of productivity and motivation.

The World card often means the closure of a particular chapter in your life, and, at the same time, the start of a new chapter. You might pull this card when you have successfully completed a goal you've been working towards or have found resolution in your life in some way. The World is letting you know that you have accomplished what you set out to do, and it is now time to embrace a new life cycle and the new growth that comes with it.

Like Capricorn knows to do, you must continue moving forward with your work and your goals. Once you have found success, give yourself something new to achieve. This will lead you to the most growth, success, and happiness.

IT'S SCORPIO SEASON: THIS IS THE TAROT CARD TO LOOK OUT FOR THIS NOVEMBER

Each zodiac sign has a tarot card associated with them. We're solidly in Scorpio season now, which means that it's time to be on the lookout for the tarot card that is most closely related to this passionate water sign.

Every zodiac sign has a related tarot card from the Major Arcana. Scorpio's tarot card is Death—an ominous yet appropriate card for the mysterious sign.

If you've seen the Death card appear frequently in your readings, here's what to know.

It could be your sun sign card

If you're a Scorpio, you might be seeing the Death card a lot because it's related to you. Sometimes, a tarot card can appear as a personal protector or advisor—this can change its meaning slightly. As a Scorpio, you might find the Death card to be reassuring. It may be appearing more often than usual because it's your birthday season—this is when your Scorpio traits truly shine, after all.

In this case, the Death card might not always appear to signify its original meaning. It may be giving you advice that is more personal to you; if the Death card seems to appear at certain times (when you need reassurance, when life changes are happening, when you need cheering up), then it may be there to remind you that you are connected to it and protected by it.

THE MONTH MAY INFLUENCE THIS CARD

Fall is a season of change. As we head into the darker months, we may retreat from ourselves more. The Death card invites you to make this a season of shedding; to allow yourself to focus on what truly works for you and leave behind the things that are burdening you. Now is an important time to release the things that are difficult to carry; the energy of summer has finally left, and it is hibernation season.

In order to properly prepare for the winter, the Death card may appear this month in particular as a reminder to cleanse yourself emotionally and mentally to prepare for the short days ahead. The Death card is very appropriate for this month in particular, and there's no one that can't use a little reminder to put self-care first as winter approaches.

KEEP THE TRADITIONAL MEANING IN MIND

The alternatives don't necessarily negate the original meaning of the Death card. If you feel that the card applies to a current situation, keep its meaning in mind: let go of what no longer serves you. This could apply to a much greater situation in your life or the card could just be asking you to take a look inward and see what thoughts are harming your life.

The Death card may be more powerful and meaningful this November, but that doesn't mean that you can't read it the same as you always would. If you don't feel personally connected to the card but feel that you can apply it to your life this month without taking the season into account, then by all means—do so. Tarot is meant to be a measure of guidance, so apply this card as it best suits you.

YOU SHOULD TRY READING TAROT CARDS THIS HALLOWEEN

For some, tarot can be a highly spiritual practice—for others, it's simply a way to connect with their inner selves and intuition. Tarot also isn't an inherently 'scary' thing—unlike what many horror movies imply, it won't curse you or actively change your future—it's more of a guide to help you live your best life.

But even if tarot itself isn't frightening, that doesn't mean Halloween isn't a great time to try it for the first time—or continue with your readings if you're an experienced user.

For one, Halloween is considered a time where magic and spirits roam free. It may make your readings feel more exciting or meaningful.

You might also feel more connected with your deck of tarot cards or find that it's easier for you to interpret the meanings of the cards you pull. When you're already in a creative mindset from the holiday itself, you might find that your interpretations become more creative, too. Additionally, the positive and fun mindset that Halloween typically brings about for most people can imbibe your tarot deck with positive energy, giving you intuitive (and possibly more accurate) readings.

Halloween is also a holiday that is associated with witches and witchcraft, though not all practicing witches celebrate it. Whether or not you have ties to witchcraft or are interested in magic, tarot cards can be a related activity—they can feel downright divine to many people, especially if tarot cards already feel spiritual to you. They don't have to be related to witchery, but they certainly can be if you find that makes them more interesting or meaningful to you.

Since Halloween is a fun and exciting holiday, you also don't need to worry about being disrespectful by practicing tarot on Halloween. Anyone can practice reading tarot, and Halloween is a great opportunity to try it out.

You'll also notice that many tarot decks become more accessible around Halloween. You might find them sold as Halloween decorations or accessories. You might also find that tarot sellers will have Halloween-related sales for anyone who was inspired to try tarot for the fall season.

Lastly, if you're a beginner learning how to read tarot for other people as well as yourself—or just want the opportunity to try practicing reading cards for others—Halloween can be a great opportunity for that, too. Other people may be more open to having a tarot reading performed as a Halloween activity. This will also give you the opportunity to practice it in a fun, low-stress setting.

AFTERWORD

I hope that this book has helped open your eyes to the wonder and joy of being a practicing zodiac. This is just the beginning of your journey; in astrology, we are always learning, growing, and discovering new things about ourselves. Do not be afraid of change, nor of new beginnings; you have your whole life ahead of you to grow into your skin and unearth who you really are. Use this book as a guide that you can return to when you need to remind yourself of what is important to you, or allow it to be a way you can reflect upon yourself from time to time. Take its lessons with you to support you throughout your daily life, just as I do for myself. I sincerely hope that these writings have helped you just as much as astrology and tarot has helped me.

Thank you for joining me on this journey to becoming a practicing zodiac. We will never know everything there is to know about life, but isn't that the true joy of it all? We can find confidence, peace, and guidance in the stars—a precious tool that has led humanity to new heights again and again for thousands of years.

I hope that, as practicing zodiacs, we are able to flourish together. I wish you growth and happiness in your future. I'm so grateful that this book fell into your hands, and I hope it makes an impact on your life in some way, however small.

Forever grateful,
Nina

*Nina Sterle is a writer and blogger
with a penchant for the cosmos.*

COLLECTIVE.WORLD/AUTHOR/NINA-STERLE

THOUGHT CATALOG Books

Thought Catalog Books is a publishing imprint of Thought Catalog, a digital magazine for thoughtful storytelling, and is owned and operated by The Thought & Expression Co. Inc., an independent media group based in the United States of America. Founded in 2010, we are committed to helping people become better communicators and listeners to engender a more exciting, attentive, and imaginative world. The Thought Catalog Books imprint connects Thought Catalog's digital-native roots with our love of traditional book publishing. The books we publish are designed as beloved art pieces. We publish work we love. Pioneering an author-first and holistic approach to book publishing, Thought Catalog Books has created numerous best-selling print books, audiobooks, and eBooks that are being translated in 40+ languages.

ThoughtCatalog.com | **Thoughtful Storytelling**

ShopCatalog.com | **Shop Books + Curated Products**

MORE FROM
THOUGHT CATALOG BOOKS

Manifesting for Beginners: A Step By Step Guide To Attracting A Life You Love
Victoria Jackson

Your Loved Ones Are Always With You: Connecting With The Other Side
Zena

How You'll Do Everything Based On Your Zodiac Sign
Chrissy Stockton

Play the Tarot Cards You're Dealt: Practical Prompts To Manifest Your Dreams
Stephanie Dempsey

Daily Dose of Magic—Card Deck
Victoria Jackson

THOUGHTCATALOG.COM

www.ingramcontent.com/pod-product-compliance
Lightning Source LLC
Chambersburg PA
CBHW031818110426
42743CB00057B/651